Africa and Europe

from Roman times
to the present

Norman R. Bennett

Africana Publishing Co. · New York and London

A Division of Holmes & Meier Publishers, Inc.

Published in the United States of America 1975 by
Africana Publishing Company
A Division of Holmes & Meier Publishers, Inc.
101 Fifth Avenue
New York, N. Y. 10003

Published in Great Britain 1975 by
Holmes & Meier Publishers, Ltd.
Hillview House
1, Hallswelle Parade, Finchley Road
London, NW 11 0DL

Library of Congress Cataloging in Publication Data

Bennett, Norman Robert, 1932-
   Africa and Europe: from Roman
times to the present.
   Bibliography: p.
   Includes index.
   1. Africa—History—To 1884. 2. Africa—History—
1884-1960. 3. Africa—Colonization. I. Title.
DT20.B46   1975   960   74-84651
ISBN 0-8419-0172-4
ISBN 0-8419-0173-2 pbk.

PRINTED IN THE UNITED STATES OF AMERICA

089203

Preface

Until the years following World War II the history of the African continent and its inhabitants usually was treated as a part of the colonial history of the expansive nation-states of Europe. The weakening of the European colonial powers caused by that war, plus the changed world scene of the postwar world, led to movements whereby most subject peoples in Africa and Asia secured their independence by the 1960s. Along with this social and political ferment came a redirection of scholarly interest concerned with the understanding of the past of the indigenous peoples of Africa, both before and during the colonial period. At the present time the history of Africa is at last being written in a fashion similar to that of other regions of the world. The focus of analysis is upon the indigenous peoples of Africa. It includes an awareness of their cultural characteristics, and most importantly, it is done with the careful study of the written, oral, and other source materials indigenous to Africa.

The purpose of this study is to utilize this recent scholarship to provide a succinct account of the relationships of Africa and Europe extending from the period before the beginning of the Christian era to the decade of the 1960s. The size of the African continent, the many differing peoples living there, and the long centuries of various European contacts necessitates following a selective approach. To provide a continuity of development certain regions of Africa have been selected for treatment throughout much of this volume, with lesser attention being given to other equally important regions, many of which follow the main lines of development of the areas included. Because of the nature of present scholarship concerning Africa, the volume deals mostly with political events, although economic, social, and other historical themes are introduced when necessary to illuminate the changing aspects of African life.

My underlying purpose has been to emphasize the many years of mutual contact between Africans and Europeans, with special emphasis upon the period from the nineteenth century when the European nations conquered most of Africa and subjected it to colonial rule. It was within the various imposed colonial systems that the leaders of present-day Africa reached maturity. Hopefully the analysis of their continent during this brief, but important, period in African history will provide some understanding of the continuing development of the new nations of Africa.

Naples and Boston
August 1972—May 1974

Acknowledgments

Several of my colleagues gave willingly of their time to read and comment upon the first drafts of this volume. Leslie C. Duly of the University of Nebraska and Douglas L. Wheeler of the University of New Hampshire commented upon the entire volume, while Daniel F. McCall, Creighton Gabel, and Louis Brenner, all of Boston Univeristy, John D. Hargreaves of the University of Aberdeen, and George E. Brooks, Jr., of Indiana University commented upon other sections. Any remaining errors remain my responsibility. I also gratefully acknowledge the able help of Frankie Healey and Jeanette Olson in preparing this work for publication.

CONTENTS

Chapter One
Africa before European Contact   **1**

Chapter Two
Africa and Europe to 1800   **19**

Roman Africa   *19*
Muslim Invasions   *24*
Portugal and Africa   *27*
Europeans in West Africa   *42*
The Dutch in South Africa   *50*

Chapter Three
Europe Conquers Africa   **55**

The Campaign against the Slave Trade   *56*
France and Egypt   *62*
Britain and South Africa   *63*
France and Senegal and Algeria   *66*
Exploring Africa: The Niger   *75*
Exploring Africa: The Nile and Congo   *78*
Explaining the Scramble   *84*
The Partition of Africa   *93*
African Reactions   *108*

Chapter Four

European Colonial Policies 123

French Colonial Policy   *125*
British Colonial Policy   *143*
Belgian Colonial Policy   *159*
Portuguese Colonial Policy   *161*
Britain and South Africa   *163*
Conclusions   *165*

Chapter Five

African Responses 167

African Rebellions   *168*
Africans and Western Education   *176*
Early Nationalist Movements   *185*
Ending the Colonial Era   *196*

Chapter Six

Conclusion 221

Bibliographical Note 225

Index 235

MAPS

African States and Peoples   8
Detail—East African Highlands   9
Limits of Roman Africa   20
European Territorial Claims in Africa—1880   94
European Territorial Claims in Africa—1914   124
Africa Today   218

1 Africa before European Contact

In the vastness of the African continent, with a maximum spread from east to west of about 4,600 miles, and a distance of over 5,000 miles between its northern and southern extremities—an area now inhabited by over 300 million people of diverse cultures and languages—it is impossible to speak of any one way of life common to its inhabitants before the coming of the Europeans. And the fact that varying numbers of the populations of different parts of Europe and Africa have been interacting with each other for many millennia further complicates efforts at generalization. Europeans, Greeks, Romans, and other Mediterranean peoples came as traders, settlers, and conquerors to intrude their cultural

1

patterns among African mores as early as the last 1,000 years before the beginning of the Chrsitian era. Furthermore, well before this period, there certainly were long centuries of intercourse between the peoples inhabiting the northern and southern shores of the Mediterranean Sea. These contacts, continuing the ever-changing patterns, endured until the twentieth century, by which time virtually all Africans had been ruled for varying periods by alien invaders or their descendants. And, naturally enough, during the course of these thousands of years, African ways of life were continually evolving, reacting in the manner common to all mankind to the specific stimuli which influenced events in every different locality. The creation, flourishing and disintegration of African political units went on much as other continents up to the fifteenth century. Then Europeans began the frenzied burst of expansion which ultimately made them the arbiters of most of mankind until their self-imposed catastrophes of 1914-18 and 1939-45 shattered irrevocably their patterns of dominance.

But until the actual military conquest of most of Africa by Europeans in the nineteenth and twentieth centuries, the continent's populations, except in regions significantly influenced by intruders from Asia, were largely left free to shape their own individual paths of development. And because of the physical configuration of the continent, especially south of the extensive Sahara Desert where good harbors were extremely rare, Africans remained for long periods of time isolated from the main centers of the evolution of modern world civilization. This, however, was not always the case. Present archaeological research indicates that the human race originated in eastern and southern Africa well over two million years ago, and spread from there to other parts of the world, where further evolution led to the populations we know today. Although, as one prominent prehistorian has cautioned, we can not yet be sure that "the transmutation from proto-hominid to man" acutally occurred in Africa, this hypothesis nevertheless remains the best conclusion until new evidence is uncovered.[1] During the millions of years of the Stone Age, the longest period of man's history, Africa reigned as the technological innovative center of the world. Its inhabitants pioneered, again in eastern and southern Africa, the development and improvement of the increasingly complex implements which allowed early man to accomplish successfully the initial mastery of his environment that was a necessary prelude to all later progress.

With the appearance of a settled agricultural civilization in the Neolithic era about 10,000 years ago in western Asia, Africa began to lose its position at the forefront of the evolution of world civilization.[2] The decline, however, was not immediate. An integral part of the early Neolithic progression was located along the narrow and fertile banks of the Nile River where the early Egyptians, profiting from the annual deposits of fertile topsoil stemming from the Blue Nile's course through the Ethiopian highlands, created one of the most highly developed of ancient civilizations. But as important as Egypt was for the later history of Africa, once its civilization took form the Egyptians became one of the most conservative of all nations, maintaining along the Nile their essential ways of life without sweeping changes for about 3,000 years. Consequently, new thrusts in the onward pro-

1. J. Desmond Clark, *The Prehistory of Africa* (New York, 1970), 45.
2. There are arguments advanced, which are generally not accepted, for an independent separate development of agriculture in Africa in Ethiopia and the western Sudanic regions.

gress of world civilization came not from Egypt but instead from centers outside of Africa.

The southern portion of the African continent, however, remained largely uninfluenced by these emerging centers and even by the valley of the Nile itself for many centuries. Geographical and other factors led to this isolation. The desert of the north hindered any easy or regular influx of ideas to the great mass of sub-Saharan African, and, though always crossed by some enterprising traders, the Sahara remained an important barrier. The coasts of Africa were also not receptive to visitors. Along the Atlantic Ocean littoral, wind patterns made access difficult until the European advances in maritime technology of the fifteenth century. Even this change did not solve the problem, since there were few good harbors. In addition, most major western African rivers were of little use for the penetration of the interior since, as on the 3,000-mile long Congo (or Zaire) River, rapids were formed as the river flowed from the elevated inland plateau. And in the case of the over 2,500-mile long Niger River, the waterway fragmented into many outlets through a great mangrove tree swamp before reaching the Atlantic Ocean, thus effectively concealing all knowledge of its outlet from outsiders until the European explorations of the nineteenth century. In eastern Africa the hazards of sea travel were mitigated by regular monsoon winds which blew from the northeast from Asia from about October to February, and from the southwest towards Asia for the rest of the year, enabling foreigners to visit this coast of Africa from a very early period. But here again, there were no navigable rivers to facilitate access to the interior across the often inhospitable territories bordering the coasts.

Other impediments to the penetration of the inland regions were even more formidable. Africa was, and is, the home of serious diseases which endanger the lives of men and animals. The tsetse fly, for example, was present throughout large areas of the continent, thus rendering impossible the use of any effective system of animal transport. (Certainly this factor was one of the principal reasons why African societies south of the Sahara never developed a system of transport utilizing the wheel.) A major region where the tsetse fly was absent, in southern Africa, was so far distant by sea from the centers of world civilization that it was not until the mid-seventeenth century that outsiders arrived to begin a settlement, from which they later penetrated deeply into the interior. The many diseases affecting man, such as malaria and yellow fever, for most of which there was no adequate treatment until the end of the nineteenth century or even later, obviously also exercised a major influence in inhibiting foreign settlement and interior penetration.

Most of Africa therefore underwent slow and measured evolution in isolation from the events occurring in the major centers of world civilization. Nevertheless, Africans were never entirely cut off from many of the important steps in man's progress taking place in areas outside of the continent. For example, after the working of iron was discovered in western Asia in the middle of the second millennium B.C., the process was brought to Egypt by the sixth or seventh century B.C. by the martial Assyrian conquerors of the Nile valley kingdom. From this region a great iron-producing civilization later developed in the state of Meroe, located within the northern area of the present-day Republic of the Sudan. Some scholars have argued that the knowledge of iron-working spread into sub-Saharan Africa from Meroe after that state's destruction by the army of the Ethiopian kingdom of Axum in the fourth century A.D. There are no sound proofs for this assertion: iron-working could equally have penetrated into Africa from Arabia, from the Phoenecian settlements along the northern Africa coast, or even from southeast Asia. But whatever the source of its origin, iron-working did appear within the borders of the present state of Nigeria, in the region between the Niger and Benue rivers inhabited by the Nok culture, by the middle of the first millennium B.C. In East Africa the knowledge of the use of this metal dates from the first to the fourth centuries of the Christian era. In any case, however unresolved the controversy over the ultimate source remains, Africans did enter the Iron Age, a period which continued in some sections of Africa until the early years of the twentieth century.

The utilization of iron made possible major advances in African civilization. One group of Africans, for example, coming to possess the vastly superior new iron implements so useful in warfare, hunting, and agriculture, spread their influence over wide regions of the continent. The ancestors of the present-day Bantu-speaking populations of Africa, originating from a nucleus in West Africa located in the region of the Niger and Benue rivers, began near the turn of the Christian era a slow and persistent process of expansion. The iron technology, possibly allied with the introduction of new food-producing crops originating from southeast Asia, such as yams and bananas, allowed the growing Bantu population to infiltrate and absorb the indigenous hunting and gathering peoples who formerly had ranged over much of Africa. Eventually the speakers of the many related Bantu languages occupied an area stretching in the north from a rough line across the continent from the Benue-Niger confluence to the mouth of the Tana River and reaching to the southern extreme of Africa, leaving an enclave of San (Bushman) and Khoikhoi (Hottentot) inhabitants in the southern zone facing the Atlantic. The effects of this vast social process were still continuing when modern Euroeans arrived in Africa.

Within this pattern of change occurring among Bantu-speakers and many others, the African peoples whom we know today began to take form. The creation of the earliest known African kingdoms in the regions south of the Sahara was one of the results of these centuries of still—and perhaps forever—obscure years of flux. Located in the western Sudanic area, these great states held sway over considerable extents of territory. By the eighth century, or even earlier, Ghana, with its capital at Kumbi-Salah, was exercising effective control over a considerable empire. Profiting from the domination of the access routes to the major gold-producing regions of West Africa, Ghana was in commercial contact with the Muslim centers of the Mediterranean world via routes across the Sahara. With the traders from the north came the Islamic religion. At first spreading among the commercial and ruling elites of Sudanic society, Islam later gained an increasing acceptance among the masses of the population. The successor states to Ghana's preeminence in the western Sudan—Mali and Songhai—both had Muslim rulers, each becoming, at least in its ruling class, an integral, albeit marginal, part of the greater Islamic world.

In eastern Africa Muslim civilization similarly exercised an important role in state development. Here traders from southern Arabia and the Persian Gulf littoral, following patterns evolved long before the seventh-century rise of Islam, intermingled with the indigenous inhabitants of the

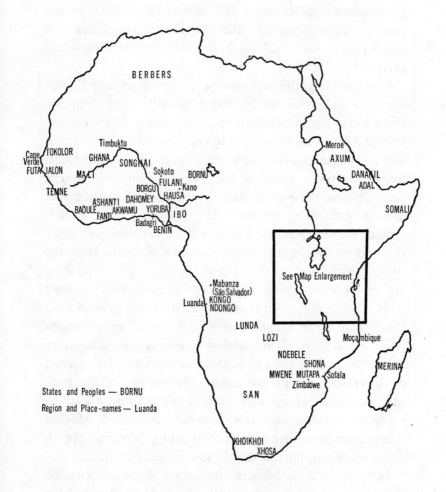

BERBERS

Cape Verde
TOKOLOR
Timbuktu
GHANA
SONGHAI
FUTA JALON
MALI
Sokoto
BORNU
FULANI
Kano
BORGU
HAUSA
TEMNE
DAHOMEY
ASHANTI AKWAMU
YORUBA
BAOULE
FANTI
IBO
Badagri
BENIN

Meroe
AXUM
DANAKIL
ADAL
SOMALI

Mabanza
(São Salvador)
Luanda
KONGO
NDONGO
LUNDA
LOZI

See Map Enlargement

NDEBELE
SHONA
MWENE MUTAPA
Zimbabwe
Sofala
Moçambique

MERINA

SAN

States and Peoples — BORNU
Region and Place-names — Luanda

KHOIKHOI
XHOSA

African States and Peoples

8

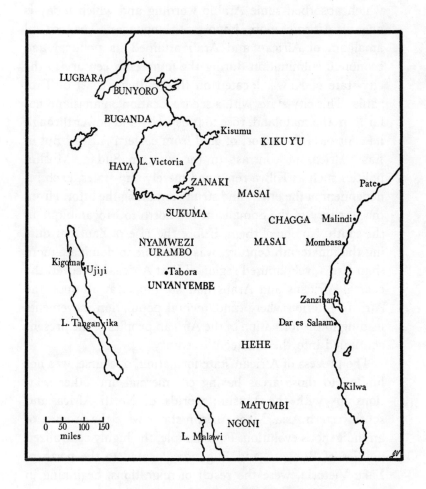

Detail—East African Highlands

eastern coast. One important result was the formation of the African populations who spoke Swahili, a Bantu language which absorbed some Arabic wording and which today is one of Africa's more important languages. The coastal amalgam of African and Arab attained its political and economic culmination during the fourteenth century in the city-state of Kilwa, located on the southern coast of Tanzania. This city-state, with a secure location on an island not far from the mainland, rose to prosperity and power through its control of the export of gold from eastern Africa.[3] But in East Africa, in contrast to the western Sudan, Muslim polities such as Kilwa remained merely city-states, each independent of the other, and strung out along the littoral from the territory of the Somalis in the north to Moçambique in the south. No one of them, before the rise of Zanzibar during the nineteenth century, was ever able to dominate more than a relatively limited region of East Africa. Moreover, the coastal Africans and Arabs had no impact at all upon the African interior where fundamental population movements leading to the formation of the African peoples of the present continued into the nineteenth century.

The process of African state formation, of course, was not limited to those areas having commercial and other relationships with the Muslim worlds of North Africa and southwestern Asia. Most African states were the product of an indigenous evolution. For example, the highly centralized polities of Bunyoro and Buganda, located to the north of Lake Victoria, were the result of migrations, beginning in about the sixteenth century, of Lwoo-speaking peoples who originated in the territories around the banks of the Nile in

3. The gold originated in the territories behind the Moçambique coast, passing to ports on that coast subject to the control of Kilwa.

the southern Sudan. The two states evolved efficiently structured forms of government with their rulers, the *mukama* in Bunyoro and the *kabaka* in Buganda, ultimately exercising powers in their societies which many observers have compared to the feudal systems of Europe.

Buganda, once it was freed from its early subordination to Bunyoro, represented one of the most highly centralized political entities to develop in Africa. Profiting from the abundant rainfall brought by its position on the elevated plateau near Lake Victoria, it had the important benefit of a secure agricultural base, of which the easily cultivated plantain was the key crop. It was thus possible for a dense population to develop in which many of the members of the society were largely free to devote their energies to political and military occupations. In a slow process which culminated after the middle years of the nineteenth century, the *kabakas,* especially the outstanding ruler Mutesa I, who ruled from 1856 to 1884, made themselves the dominant political directors of their society. The state of Buganda was divided into counties, each administered by an official who presided over a hierarchy reaching down to the village chiefs. All officials were responsible to the superior directly above them in the hierarchy. Further control from the central government was insured by the fact that most chiefs, at all levels of the administration, were appointed directly by the *kabaka*, and were also subject to transfer or dismissal at his will. The possession of land, a vital component of the system, was regulated in terms of the individual's, and the official's, relationship to his superiors. An additional guarantee of obedience was attained by the appointment of other officials throughout the administrative system who observed events and reported directly concerning them to the *kabaka*. Thus virtually all officials owed their appointment to office and the continuation of their functions to the will of their sovereign (even the heads of the clans of Buganda needed his confirmation), while practically every detail of the workings of the administration was subordinate to his regulation.

This analysis is naturally idealized, since every ruler had to deal with the power blocks existing within his society which had to be satisfied. The *kabaka*, for example, was selected from among those individuals whose father or grandfather had been *kabaka* by the chief minister of the Ganda state, the *katikiro*, and other senior chiefs. Consequently, this group, and especially the *katikiro*, often possessed extensive influence in the new ruler's administration. Additionally, the *kabaka* never controlled an effective standing army, thus rendering his rule even more dependent upon the support received from his chief subordinates. But despite these handicaps, the *kabaka* had largely mastered the dynamics of administrative control until, during the last quarter of the nineteenth century, the incursions of Arabs and Europeans upset the mechanisms of Ganda society. In West Africa, the small but powerful state of Dahomey, along with many other states, had a similarly centralized administration during the nineteenth century, with its ruler equally controlling the activities of his civil and religious functionaries.

Historians of Africa have, however, often placed excessive stress on the more centrally organized states. Such polities have proved to be the easiest to deal with in matters of historical reconstruction, possessing as they often did extended king lists and other traditions preserved in oral form which allowed a more straightforward interpretation of their past. Many Africans, including some of the most historically significant of the continent's peoples, nonetheless lived their lives at the other extreme of the political spectrum as part of what are sometimes called "states without rulers." One such African people, for example, the Lugbara of northern Uganda, regulated their affairs in lineage councils where open discussions, the important weight of their elders' thoughts, and the resulting force of public opinion formed the effective binding force of political life. Africans living in societies of this type often had a narrow focus, dealing largely with the affairs revolving around their homesteads or villages, leaving the problems of broader import to other discussions, generally similar in format to the local councils, held between the various scatttered settlements of the entire culture group.

Peoples with populations numbering in the millions effectively conducted their lives utilizing such decentralized institutions. The vigorous Ibo peoples of southern Nigeria, with a total population by the 1960s of over 5 million individuals, settled in areas where the density of population was at times over 1,000 persons per square mile, are perhaps the best known example of the intricate forms of government which flourished under a decentralized system of political rule. The Ibo, who were probably not conscious until the twentieth century of being members of a greater cultural entity designated as "Igbo," had in their over 200 separate groupings varying forms of organization, even including some forms of centralized government in regions where they had been influenced by the important neighboring state of Benin. More typical, however, was the organization of the Ibo living in acephalous groups. In these individualistic and egalitarian societies all male members had the opportunity to rise in status and wealth through the exercise of their particular talents. They belonged to hundreds of patrilineal clans, with numbers ranging from 5,000 to 15,000 individuals, each possessing its own distinct customs. The clans resided in villages, the basic unit of the political system. Among the Afikpo Ibo, for example, a grouping encompassing over twenty villages, the men were divided into age grades which regulated their society's affairs. The individuals between the ages of sixty-five and eighty-three legislated for the entire Afikpo group, while the age grade including those between the ages of fifty-five and sixty-four carried out their elder's rulings which had been arrived at in open councils. In individual villages, the sixty-five to eighty-three-year-old age grade held most influence, but other elder grades also participated in decisions. All adult males had a right to join the elders in discussions and all had a right to speak. This form of government, so foreign to the experience of most of the European invaders of Africa, caused special problems during the later colonial era. Some of the countless variations between the political extremes of the organizations of the Ganda and the Ibo will be examined during the course of this volume.

Most Africans busied themselves with gaining a livelihood thorugh agricultural pursuits, stock-rearing, or a combination of both. The soils of Africa are notably deficient, and lacking either effective agricultural implements or suitable fertilizers, many African cultivators practiced a "slash and burn" technique by which plots were cleared of natural vegetation and other hindrances to cultivation. After varying periods of use the plots were left to regain their fertility through natural processes while the cultivators moved on to clear new fields. Since until relatively recently the population of the African continent was limited, there was normally ample land available for the shifting patterns of agriculture, and the consequent problems stemming from land overuse, such as erosion, were not a serious concern. Depending upon the particular region of the continent, the rainfall, and many other relevant factors, African farmers cultivated grains, root crops and plantains among their major crops. Except in a few favored regions, as in Buganda or upon the slopes of Mount Kilimanjaro inhabited by the numerous Chagga peoples, where abundant rainfall insured yearly surpluses, many Africans lived an often uncertain existence under the recurring threat of drought and famine. Their limited technologies did not allow for the collection of a crop surplus as insurance against hard times. In any case they possessed no adequate storage facilities for such surpluses. This was a lasting problem, unfortunately remaining unresolved throughout the years of the colonial era. Even today, when modern means of transport are often available, it still adversely effects some African populations.

Other Africans organized their lives around the keeping of livestock. The Masai of East Africa with their cattle, or the Somali of the Horn of Africa with their camels, both practicing politically decentralized forms of government, ranged over wide areas during the appropriate seasons in search of adequate pasturage and water for their herds. Both the Somali and Masai lived off of the products of their animals and not the animals themselves; they were killed for eating, however, for ceremonial occasions, or when they were about to die from natural or accidental causes. Livestock-owning peoples like the Masai and Somali often expressed disdain for settled agriculturalists, but nonetheless they required at least some agricultural products. Therefore a regular commerce was usually carried on between pastoralists and sedentary populations to satisfy the requirements of each group. Cattle also formed a vital basis of life for Africans who did not follow the pastoral way of livelihood. In some African societies, notably those dominated by the Tutsi peoples of the Central African states of Rwanda and Burundi, cattle were the focus of all significant societal activities, with virtually all social values expressed in terms relating to them, and with political loyalties largely based upon their distribution by the dominant, cattle-holding class among their subordinates. But this "cattle complex" was not universal either among pastoralists or more settled populations. Other Africans maintained herds, in the manner more familiar to Europeans, as useful adjuncts to what was gained from the soil for supplying the nutritional needs of their societies.

Because of the difficulties of furnishing regular supplies of foodstuffs to large numbers of people, urban centers usually did not play a predominant role in most sections of Africa. There simply was not present an advanced enough technology to nourish adequately a large population living any considerable distance from the food-producing regions of each locality. Most urban centers, at least by modern standards, contained very limited populations. The East African coastal entrepôt of Kilwa, for example, probably had a population of from 4,000 to 10,000 inhabitants at the beginning of the sixteenth century (although the number probably had been larger in the middle of the fourteenth century during its most flourishing period), a number which could be conveniently supported from nearby agricultural areas. Similarly, the great walled city of Kano, in northern Nigeria, a Hausa commercial and industrial center, had about 30,000 inhabitants by the middle of the nineteenth century. Other cities, of a very different pattern, developed among the Yoruba peoples of western Nigeria. The Yoruba agriculturalists resided in urban conglomerations, but they left them daily to labor in their fields. The situation was somewhat different in northern Africa where there had been a few extremely significant urban settlements from the time of Carthage (c.800 B.C.). But Carthage, with an estimated population in the hundreds of thousands, and its Northern African successors, great maritime and commercial centers, as well as important administrative centers such as that which grew at Cairo after 969, were not typical. The very many cities of northern Africa which flourished during and after the period of Roman rule were as dependent upon the neighboring countryside as their counterparts in Africa south of the Sahara.

The foregoing analysis has indicated that the great number and diversity of the peoples and systems of life within Africa precludes the success of any brief attempt to portray the Africa which existed, at varying times over a period of thousands of years, before the era of intensive European contact. Most Africans lived in a manner similar to that of the other inhabitants of the common world community existing in the days before the traumatic changes brought by the Industrial Revolution. Most labored in their own limited neighborhoods with scant concern for the events occurring in distant—or not so distant—places. Sometimes states of differing organizations were superimposed upon the masses engaged in the steady toil of subsistence economies, varying from the forms represented in the Christian kingdom of Ethiopia, the Muslim state of Bornu in Northern Nigeria, or the African polity of the Lunda peoples of Central Africa. Apart from them were the wandering pastoralists of Africa living in societies which, like some of their settled agricultural compatriots, lacked strong chiefly office. Such peoples, like the Berbers of northern Africa, or the Fulani of West Africa, nevertheless often possessed the strength to overrun the territories of their more centrally organized neighbors. But no matter what their political organization or manner of livelihood, all Africans sooner or later had to redesign their ways of life to either resist or tolerate the European nations who by the middle of the twentieth century had succeeded in conquering virtually all of the African continent.

2 Africa and Europe to 1800

Roman Africa

Europeans began to rule parts of Africa long before the hectic years of the scramble for the territorial control of the continent beginning in the 1880s. The earliest significant European conquerors of African peoples were the Romans.They were initially drawn into occupying the coastal regions west of Egypt because of their long and always difficult military contest with the African-based empire of Carthage for the mastery of the western Mediterranean world. The great city of Carthage, founded according to

19

tradition in about 800 B.C., was located near the modern center of Tunis. Its citizens dominated an extensive state which at varying periods encompassed lands in North Africa, Sicily, Sardinia, and Spain. The ruling Carthaginians, a Semitic-speaking people descended from immigrants originating in the important Phoenician city of Tyre, were among the foremost commercial entrepreneurs of the ancient Mediterranean world. By unceasing mercantile diligence, and through an often ruthless suppression of their rivals, the Carthaginians had succeeded in creating a flourishing commercial and industrial civilization supported by a prosperous agricultural North African base. Their achievements, however, were significant only in the economic sphere. They never attempted to be anything but an alien people ruling over the indigenous populations of North Africa.

By the third century B.C. the rising and aggressive Roman Republic, which had earlier necessarily accepted commercial treaties placing Rome in a subordinate position to the North African state, was becoming increasingly ready to exercise its

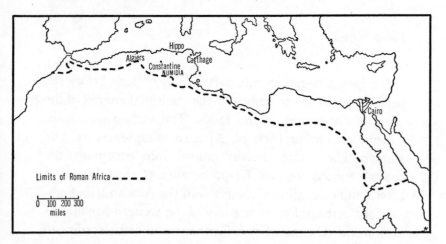

Limits of Roman Africa — — —

0   100 200 300
       miles

formidable military strength against Carthage. When a test of strength came about over the Sicilian city of Messina, located on the strategic strait between Sicily and the Italian peninsula, the Romans resolved to challenge Carthage. The ensuing hostilities, the First Punic War (264-241 B.C.), resulted in a major defeat for Carthage and the loss of its strategically vital holdings in Sicily which had allowed the control of the routes of Mediterranean commerce. Carthaginian efforts to regain their lost power, particularly in Spain, led to new hostilities. But in the Second Punic War (218-202 B.C.), despite the military genius of the great Carthaginian leader Hannibal, Rome once more triumphed. The harsh terms of the peace settlement imposed upon Carthage left its remaining North African territories threatened by the expansive policies of a vigorous African ally of Rome, the Berber state-builder Massinissa. When this wily ruler's aggressions forced the Carthaginians to fight to defend their continued existence as an independent state, the Romans declared war. In a frenzy of unrestrained demonstration of their military strength, the Romans and their African allies completely destroyed the city of their once formidable rivals in 146 B.C.

The destruction of Carthage, however, was not a sensible action, since the city's vital strategic location on the major east-west Mediterranean sea route left a vacuum which had to be refilled. After some minor rebuilding ventures, the Romans during the reign of Augustus (27 B.C.-14 A.D.) began a major effort designed to re-create the once-great city. In subsequent years a significant policy of colonization by the Romans made their North African provinces, which expanded from the territory around Carthage to reach a maximum extent in the fourth century, one of the most prosperous segments of their world empire. Meanwhile Egypt, which had been conquered by Alexander the Great in the fourth century B.C., and had subseqently been ruled by the dynasty of the Ptolemies, fell to Rome in the first century B.C. The flourishing agricultural production of both North African segments of the Roman Empire made them the vital suppliers of foodstuffs for the growing and increasingly unruly population of the Roman capital city.

In Egypt the Romans built their administration upon the foundation of the existing well-elaborated bureaucracy. But in their effort to colonize and administer the western territories of the North African littoral, much of which had been very lightly, if at all, administered from Carthage, the Romans inaugurated imperial policies which remain of interest because they were the precursors of techniques of ruling alien populations later adopted by the more recent rulers of Africa. Under the Roman Empire, effective participation in political affairs was rendered possible to an individual by his attainment of citizenship in one of the empire's urban centers. Since North Africa underwent a steady urban development, more and more of its inhabitants, including many indigenous North Africans, gained this distinction, a process which culminated with the Roman Emperor Caracalla's Edict of 212. This act gave citizenship to most free men of the Roman world. It was significant that Caracalla was the son of Septimius Severus, the first North African-born Roman emperor, who ruled from 193 to 211. This policy of assimilation of indigenous peoples into the Roman polity required the individual to gain a knowledge of the Latin language and of Roman political forms so that he might successfully carry out the obligations of citizenship. As a result, North Africans were at times able to attain dominant positions in many avenues of endeavor in the Roman world. Septimius Severus and his dynasty were clearly the high point of this influence, but many other North Africans in all walks of life reached positions of distinction. The most famous undoubtedly was the seminal Christian leader Augustine, fifth-century bishop of the North African city of Hippo. Lesser citizens of the empire lived scattered throughout North Africa, managing their prosperous estates and exercising their political rights in the many towns which flourished while Rome remained powerful.

Nonetheless, despite this apparently successful winning of North African allegiance to the empire, the Roman practitioners of assimilation met the same problems as the later European followers of similar policies. The Romans only managed to find a place in their ruling society for a very narrow elite of indigenous resprentatives. The overwhelming mass of the local population remained wedded to the culture and language of their birth.

At the same time they were ruthlessly exploited by the governing sector in order to perpetrate an alien domination which often gave them few tangible benefits. Consequently revolts against Roman rule became increasingly frequent. The most important movement of social protest centered around a quarrel within the vigorous Christian community of North Africa. Through a variant interpretation of Christianity, which rejected the reintegration into their faith of members who had lapsed during periods of Roman persecution, some of the North African masses found an ideological expression for their dissent. Called Donatism, àfter Donatus, a fourth-century bishop of Numidia, the movement was eventually suppressed only with the greatest of difficulty. The unrest also occurred while the general inability of the Roman government to hold together a world empire was becoming apparent in North Africa. By the fifth century this steady decline allowed European barbarian invaders, the Vandals, to wrest the western regions of North Africa from Roman control without difficulty. The new conquerors, with their capital at Carthage, never were able to form an integrated amalgam with the indigenous North Africans or with the subjugated Roman community. After a century of Vandal rule, the Eastern Romans (Byzantines) easily conquered the North African state during the rule of Justinian in the middle of the sixth century. But the Byzantines, who also had been in control of Egypt since the end of the fourth century, never found it within their power to reconstitute the once extensive Roman holdings in western North Africa in the face of a growing opposition by the indigenous populations. Neither were the Byzantines able, largely because of difficulties arising from their interpretation of Christianity, to win the loyalties of the indigenous Coptic Christian peoples of Egypt.

Muslim Invasions

When the Muslim Arab invaders of the seventh century arrived in North Africa they relatively quickly swept away most traces of the many centuries of Roman rule. Later conquerors of African peoples, especially the French, often described themselves as the heirs to the Romans, but while they talked of assimilationist policies as one of the virtues of their rule, they nevertheless practiced them in a manner which demonstrated that they had learned little from the shortcomings of the Roman experience. In the end their colonies suffered the same fate as those of Rome.

The inspired warriors of the new Muslim empire, motivated by a combination of religious fervor and desire for booty, had completed their conquest of the coast of North Africa by the beginning of the eighth century. It took many more centuries to achieve the final Islamic conquest, both geographical and spiritual, over the territories and peoples of North Africa, but in the end the conquest was definitive. Eventually only ruined cities and country homes remained to mark the period of Roman rule. Africa was henceforth starkly separated from Europe by a Muslim belt of territory stretching from the Atlantic shore of Morocco to the Red Sea coast of Egypt. Its southern extent gradually widened as the intruding followers of Muhammad's message moved southward into the Sudanic regions. The separation was of long duration and it had important consequences. When the Roman Empire disintegrated, Europe turned inward to absorb and assimilate its barbarian invaders. Most of the previously regular contacts across the Mediterranean were forgotten. The essentially separate development of the African and European continents did not cease for practically a millennium, until the rising nation states of Western Europe began to open sea routes which led to their gain of a new influence in Africa, the Americas, and Asia.

Some contact, of course, was continually maintained between Africa and Europe, notably in commerce between cities on both sides of the Mediterranean, or less happily through the wars between Christians and Muslims which long characterized the Mediterranean scene. North African recruits to the early onward-moving Muslim tide of conquest participated in the eighth-century invasion of the Iberian peninsula. (Gibraltar derives its name from a Berber general commanding the forces which crossed the eight-mile strait which divides the two continents.) The Islamic presence in the peninsula, and the resulting natural ties to the fellow Muslims of North Africa, endured for about 800 years. The Moroccan-based dynasties of the al-Murabitun (Almoravids), al-Muwahhidun (Almohads), and Marinids conquered and ruled varying areas of the Iberian peninsula during the periods stretching from the eleventh to the fifteenth centuries. Since the Spanish Muslims then possessed one of the Islamic world's leading civilizations, they were able to make a considerable cultural impact upon the ruder Muslims of western North Africa. Europeans in turn invaded Africa, although they never achieved results equal to the Iberian conquests. The Norman kingdom in Sicily held posts in the territories opposite to its island home during the twelfth century until they were expelled by the al-Muwahhidun. The era of the Christian crusades against Islam was marked in Africa by the unsuccessful thirteenth-century expeditions of France's Louis IX against the Egypt of Salah al-Din (Saladin) and the Tunisia of the Hafsid dynasty. And despite the continuing friction between Muslim and Christian, a few Christian missionaries attempted to work in North Africa; members of the Fransiscan and Dominican orders were present during the thirteenth and fourteenth centuries. But apart from these limited northern contacts, Africa's peoples were left to develop their own destinies, either through adaptions of the steadily advancing monotheism of Islam or, more commonly, through developments stemming from within the traditional African way of life.

If Africans were unaware of the significant themes of political, social, and economic evolution occurring within

Europe, ignorance of Africa was no less great among Europeans. Africa had become an unknown territory—what Henry Morton Stanley later strikingly called the Dark Continent—with knowledge of it frozen at the level of the not very well informed geographers and other scholars of the Greek and Roman worlds. Later imperfect additions to this scholarship were accomplished—although few were able to read them—through the works of Arabic-speaking writers and travellers. Not until the beginning years of the twentieth century did Europeans and Americans complete the basic explorations which gave geographical certainty to the topography of Africa. Because of the enduring blight of the expanding European racism of the nineteenth and twentieth centuries, the quest for the understanding of African cultures is still underway.

Portugal and Africa

The principal reawakening of European interest in Africa came from the venturesome mariners of the small kingdom of Portugal, a state still fired in the fifteenth century by the Christian combative zeal which had enabled it to expel the last of its Muslim conquerors during the thirteenth century. But the struggle against the Muslim enemy did not cease with Portuguese independence. Additional Muslim states were only the distance of the Straits of Gibraltar away. Acting as crusaders for their faith with the same integral mixture of worldly and spiritual motives which their earlier Christian predecessors had brought to the Holy Land, the Portuguese carried the war into Africa. In 1415 Portugal seized the Moroccan Mediterranean port of Ceuta as her first major foothold on enemy soil. Following this successful beginning, Portugal captured a series of coastal cities extending southward along the Atlantic coast from the weak rulers of Morocco. However, most of these conquests were of limited political significance, since only the ports, and not their hinterlands, were in Portuguese hands. Many of these centers, surrounded by hostile populations, were soon regarded by their occupying garrisons as little better than prisons so that no effective contact was possible between Christian and Muslim. Perhaps the most important result of the Portuguese limited occupation was the stimulation which this Christian presence gave to the Muslims of Morocco through the vigorous leadership of the new Sa'dian dynasty. The Sa'dians were able to drive most of the Portuguese from their territory by the mid-sixteenth century.

Of far greater importance than the conquest of Muslim Ceuta was the presence at that victorious seige of young Prince Henry of Portugal. Following the conquest of the Moroccan city he resolved to divert to his nation the profitable gold trade carried on between the western Sudan and the North African littoral via the caravan routes crossing the Sahara. It has been estimated that from the eighth century to the discovery of the New World the West African gold-producing regions were the principal suppliers of this metal to Europe. The chance to turn this flow of gold to Portugal's advantage helped to provide the motivation for the series of exploratory voyages that Prince Henry, called the Navigator, dispatched southward to find a route along the unknown Atlantic coast of Africa. Other compelling reasons for the voyages were the opportunity to discover a new route, bypassing the Mediterranean, to the fabulously rich and spice-producing islands of the East; to spread the Christian faith to hitherto unreached populations; and to find new allies—especially the legendary Chrisitian ruler known as Prester John—for use in the wars against the Muslims. Prince Henry, who never himself participated in the voyages, gathered around him the most talented mariners, geographers, cartographers, and other experts skilled in the techniques of distant exploration to carry forward a slow process of penetration into regions hitherto unknown to Europeans. New advances in maritime technology, in the construction of sailing vessels, in the rigging and manipulation of sails, in the use of the compass and other aids to navigation, and in seaborne armament, contributed to Portuguese success. By 1434 Prince Henry's mariner, Gil Eannes, had succeeded in passing the dangerous reefs of Cape Bojador, and by 1460, the year of Henry's death, Portuguese vessels had sailed as far as Sierra Leone. After a short lapse, the Portuguese resumed their advance, in 1469 awarding to the merchant Fernão Gomes a five-year monopoly of the trade of the African coast beyond Cape Verde on the condition that he explore an additional 400 miles to the south each year. Gomes's concession was extended, and by 1475 the equator had been passed. Thereafter the steady Portuguese advance along the African coast continued under state supervision, marked by such important events as Diogo Caõ's discovery of the mouth of the Congo River in 1482 or 1483 and the successful voyage of Bartholemeu Dias around the southern Cape of Africa in 1487. Prince Henry's vision was realized when in the years 1497-99 the domineering voyager Vasco da Gama triumphally sailed past the Cape of Good Hope and then northward along the eastern African coasts, with stops at Moçambique,

Mombasa, and Malindi, to arrive finally at the Indian port of Calicut.

Portugal, then a nation of about one million inhabitants, soon bore the burdensome responsibility of staffing an empire and directing an extensive commerce in territories which reached from Brazil through Africa, India, and the East Indies to China and Japan. In the scale of relative profits to be gained in overseas endeavor, both for the kingdom and the individual, this extensive empire left African regions well down on the Portuguese list of imperial priorities. Nevertheless, although Africa did not become a primary theater of early Portuguese settlement or conquest, the Portuguese did have a significant impact in several areas of Africa. More importantly, the Portuguese inaugurated the first active period of political and cultural interaction between African and European since the era of Roman rule in North Africa, and it was the first such experience for the peoples of Black Africa.

The relationship between Portuguese and African, as might be expected, varied according to the relative strength of the African polity concerned, and according to what specific goals each sought from the other. A relatively minimal form of involvement was typified by the Portuguese establishments along the Gold Coast (modern Ghana) where the difficulties of passing through the heavy surf necessitated land bases. Despite opposition from the Akan-speaking inhabitants of this region, a fort, São Jorge da Mina, was begun in 1482. This settlement, as was the case with later Portuguese forts, was entirely devoted to the commercial endeavor of drawing to it much of the gold which had formerly passed northward from West Africa across the Sahara Desert. Portuguese success is indicated by the fact that by the last years of the fifteenth century about 3,000 pounds of gold annually were reaching the Portuguese kingdom. Although the Portuguese held São Jorge da Mina and their other forts until the Dutch conquered them during the seventeenth century, their European residents made very little impact upon the surrounding African populations. Each group concentrated its energies upon commerce; whatever limited cultural interaction occurred between African and European usually happened when Africans left their own areas to live within the jurisdiction of the European settlements.

Afro-European relationships were far different in the Kongo Kingdom. After the vessels of the explorer Diogo Cão reached the mouth of the Congo River the Portugese captain inaugurated regular contacts with the inhabitants of the Kongo state. In about 1485 Cão left four emissaries in the Kongo and in exchange brought four Kongolese to Portugal. They received a favorable reception and returned with Cão to their homeland in 1487, thus beginning a period of intense interaction, on many levels, between Portuguese and Kongolese. If it had been successful, the relationship could have been of great significance for the future unfolding of the encounter between Europe and Africa.

The Kongo Kingdom, located to the south of the lower Congo River and extending southward into modern Angola, was at the end of the fifteenth century an efficiently organized state, made up of six major divisions, with a capital at Mabanza (later known as São Salvador). The Kongolese king was in effective control of his administration, sharing the details of rule with provincial and district subordinates who owed their appointments to him. When the Portuguese arrived, the Kongolese ruler, Nzinga Kuwu, who ruled from

1481 to 1495, regarded himself as a sovereign equal in rank to the king of Portugal, and he was at first so treated by the Portuguese. Nzinga Kuwu was impressed by what he had learned of the newly intruding European civilization and from the 1490s a period of extended cultural borrowing began. The Kongolese ruler dispatched an embassy to Portugal to seek missionary and technical aid which returned in 1491 with some Portuguese. Nzinga Kuwu was baptized, taking the name of João I, followed by most of his nobility although he did not turn out to be long interested in Christianity. The process of interaction intensified under one of Nzinga Kuwu's successors, Mbemba Nzinga. Better known to posterity as Affonso I, he was a sovereign of considerable talent and energy, ruling from 1506 to about 1545. Christianity, in which Affonso was a sincere believer, became the state religion, while Portuguese customs, including the use of Portuguese titles and language, came into use at his court. The mass of the population, especially those individuals living at a distance from the courts of the ruler and his principal subordinates, of course continued to follow their traditional ways. Nevertheless an essential beginning had been made in the blending of European elements into the Africa lifestyle.

But unfortunately for the subjects of Affonso I and his successors, most of the interest in constructive change came from the Kongolese side. The Portuguese, with their worldwide commerical and political commitments, had scant resources, either in manpower or materiel, to spare for the relatively minor Kongo Kingdom. And, tragically, the one commodity which interested some Portuguese in the African state eventually doomed the new relationships between the two countries to failure. The nearby Atlantic Ocean island of

São Tomé, first reached by the Portuguese in 1473, early had developed a sugar plantation economy which depended for its prosperity upon the continuous importation of slaves from the African mainland. Edicts of 1486 and 1493 had established the islanders' rights to this trade. Thus during Affonso's reign, and especially after his death, Portuguese slave traders intervened with increasing frequency in the dynastic and other squabbles occurring within the Kongo. This harmful situation was made the more acute since the Kongolese state, like most African kingdoms, had no well-regulated method of succession to the throne. Many candidates were always eligible, with the consequent formation of contesting factions providing the slave traders ample opportunities for profitable interference.

Complaints by Kongolese rulers to Lisbon about the excesses of Portuguese subjects brought little effective response. At best the African rulers received only sporadic and ineffective aid to help stabilize their country. The Kongolese Kingdom gradually disintegrated, with more and more of its subordinate entities gaining an uncertain independence, until by the eighteenth century only a memory—which never died—remained of the formerly flourishing African state. The once significant contact between African and European had foundered upon the insatiable demand for slaves to supply the plantation economy of São Tomé. An enduring pattern had been established for the ensuing period of increasing search for African slaves for the successor plantations to São Tomé in the New World.

The Portuguese had begun similar relations with other African states. They had initially demonstrated a strong interest in the powerful state of Benin, located along the eastern Nigerian coast. In the latter part of the fifteenth century slave traders, pepper merchants, and missionaries resided within the kingdom, particularly at its port of Ughoto, from 1485 to about 1505. Possibly because the Portuguese were unable to dominate events in Benin, as they did in the Kongo Kingdom, they gradually lost interest in remaining in that state. The Warri polity of the Itsekiri people, to the south of Benin, was also influenced by Europeans, especially Roman Catholic missionaries, from the sixteenth to the eighteenth centuries. The new religion, however, affected only the court circles, eventually disappearing without leaving much of a legacy.

Meantime interested Portuguese became concerned with the territory located behind the coast of Angola. The Ndongo state—the modern designation of Angola derives from that of the Ngola, its ruler—which was then subordinate to the Kongo Kingdom, had drawn the attention of slave traders who were ready to support its desires for independence from its northern sovereign. With rival Portuguese fighting on both the Kongo and Ndongo sides, the Ndongo achieved their independence through battle in 1556. Other Portuguese also had been interested in establishing themselves in this region. In 1571 Paulo Dias de Novaes, with Jesuit support, was awarded a government charter (donatário) empowering him to attempt the creation of a Portuguese territory under his direction. In 1575 the founding of Luanda, Portuguese Angola's future capital, marked the beginning of the venture. The pattern of initial cooperation practiced with Africans in the Kongo was never attempted in Angola. The Portuguese relied upon their military strength, plus that of their African allies, to gradually, and often with great difficulty, extend their influence into the interior. The economic mainstay of this always unruly colony, the first large European establishment in Africa, became the export of slaves to the Portuguese possessions in the New World. Little alternate effort ever was made by either the Lisbon government or the Portuguese of Angola to modify this "single crop" dependence until the nineteenth century. Even then the Portuguese were the last of the European powers holding colonies in Africa to take significant steps against the slave trade and slavery. The Portuguese record in Angola remains one of the harshest of all the European rulers of African peoples. One can but concur with the recent judgment of Central Africa's leading historian: "From the point of view of the African subject, Angola was sheer terror."[1]

On the east coast of Africa, where by the beginning of the sixteenth century a flourishing Afro-Arab commercial civilization reigned, the Portuguese followed a different policy. Their comparatively advanced maritime military technology allowed the Portuguese *conquistadores* quickly to reduce the many independent Afro-Arab city-states to a subordinate position. Uprisings against Portuguese overlordship were frequent—the city of Mombasa was a persistently stubborn foe—but there never was any chance of long-range Afro-Arab success unless they had the cooperation of an outside power strong enough to match the Portuguese. There was no possibility of such support during the sixteenth and early seventeenth centuries; the decisive Portuguese victory over a Muslim fleet at Diu in 1509 gave them clear dominance over the waters of the western Indian Ocean for a century. Thus the Portuguese were able to hold the eastern coast of Africa and to dominate its limited commerce with a very minimal occupying force, usually numbering only in the hundreds, until they were successfully challenged at the very

1. Jan Vansina, *Kingdoms of the Savanna* (Madison, 1966), p. 147.

end of the seventeenth century by a new rival, the Arabs of Oman, in combination with the Afro-Arabs of the coast.

The main policy objective of the Portuguese in eastern Africa was to control the gold trade from the interior which had once been the monopoly of Kilwa. A fort was constructed at Sofala (located to the south of the present center of Beira) in 1505. But the oppressive policies which the Portuguese enforced upon the African and Arab participants in the inland trade to the regions of the present Rhodesia, where the great African state of the Mwene Mutapa (Monomotapa), the architect of some of the impressive stone buildings of Zimbabwe, was located, were never very successful. To combat the Arab and African hindrance to their commerce, the Portuguese in the sixteenth century attempted to reach the sources of the gold trade. One of the earliest of European missionaries to travel into the African interior, the Jesuit Gonçalo de Silveira, reached the Mwene Mutapa and succeeded in making that ruler accept Christianity. The notables of the court also follwed his example. But Silveira's success was temporary; the intrigues of Arab traders led to the missionary's death in 1561. The killing of Silveira, however, provided sufficient excuse for a military invasion of the interior, but the expeditions of 1571 and 1574 failed due to the distances involved and to the problems caused by disease faced by Europeans in east and central Africa.

Nevertheless the Portuguese during the seventeenth century were able to take advantage of internal crises within the Mwene Mutapa state and thus to hasten its disintegration as an effective African polity. But the desired commercial prosperity the Portuguese sought never materialized. In 1629 the ruler Mavura Mhande gained office because of Portuguese support. In return for the acceptance of Portuguese sovereignty, Mavura Mhande promised to pay tribute, open trade, accept Christianity, and expel Arab traders. But the deposed ruler, Nyambo Kapararidze, led an uprising soon after 1629 through which he successfully regained the throne. In this serious defeat the Portuguese lost over 300 men, and subseqently were never able to regain their former position. The Portuguese holdings, centered from 1507 at the island city of Moçambique, provided a useful supplying place for their fleets voyaging to India, from which eastern Africa was usually administered. Portuguese hopes for drawing extensive profits from the African interior, however, were never attained.

To the north of Moçambique, the Portuguese position came to center upon the port of Mombasa. When outside enemies, such as the Egyptian-backed sea raider Ali Bey, intervened during the latter part of the sixteenth century, thus stimulating the latent hostility of the Afro-Arabs, the Portuguese reacted with great ruthlessness to defeat him and to discourage further uprisings. To protect against future threats from the north, the great fortress of Fort Jesus was begun in Mombasa in 1593. But complete security for Portuguese interests was never attained. One clear example of this failure was the career of Ahmad bin Husayn, a Muslim puppet given the rule of the Afro-Arabs of Mombasa in the early seventeenth century. Educated in Portuguese India, where he had converted to Christianity, Ahmad bin Husayn nonetheless turned out to be a danger to his Portuguese sovereigns. Like many of the Africans of a later era, he was placed in an impossible position. Ahmad bin Husayn was distrusted by the Portuguese of Mombasa because of his Muslim origins, while at the same time the Muslim inhabitants of his city reacted against his efforts to carry on policies inspired by the Portuguese. Thus trapped, Ahmad bin Husayn revolted against his European masters in 1631, driving them from Mombasa. But realizing that he could not successfully contest the inevitable Portuguese counterexpedition from their Indian power base, the Arab rebel evacuated Mombasa before his enemies returned, spending his remaining years in a futile opposition to the Portuguese supremacy of the Indian Ocean.

Despite this easy victory, Portuguese dominance of their overextended African dominions was on the wane. The Afro-Arabs of the coast had sought support from the martial Omani Arabs of southeastern Arabia in the 1650s, and after several inconclusive raiding ventures, these relentless opponents of the Portuguese dispatched a large force to besiege Fort Jesus in 1696. The continuing support of the Portuguese by elements of the indigenous population, which was a principal explanation for the length of Portuguese rule in eastern Africa, now failed. Fort Jesus although ably defended by the Portuguese and their Afro-Arab allies fell after an epic seige in 1698. Despite a few futile countermeasures of the early eighteenth century, Portugese dominion north of the present territory of Moçambique was ended. The era of initial Portuguese rule in eastern Africa had provided few positive benefits for the indigenous inhabitants apart from the introduction, here as in western Africa, of valuable New World crops such as maize and cassava. Their limited physical presence had precluded any significant cutural impact, and the Portuguese invaders are best remembered for their disruptive influence on the hitherto prosperous commercial civilization of the eastern coast of Africa.

A final example of Portuguese relationships with Africans occurred in the Christian kingdom of Ethiopia, a state of potential interest to the Portuguese since it had come, largely through its adherence to Christianity, to be considered as the homeland of the fabled Prester John. The long-lived Ethiopian state traced the origins of its ruling dynasty back to the issue of a union between Solomon and Sheba. The ruler Ezana had accepted Christianity during the fourth century when the kingdom was governed from Axum. Later circumstances connected with the expansion of Islam along the littoral of the Red Sea had forced the Christian Ethiopians to withdraw into the up to 8,000-foot high broken plateau of the interior where, through amalgamation with the indigenous populations, the character of the later Ethiopian state developed. By the fourteenth and fifteenth centuries the Muslim states among the Somali and Danakil peoples living near the coast had evolved into a series of formidable polities, notably that of Adal. An intense period of conflict between Muslim and Christian led to the emergence of a charismatic Muslim leader from Adal, Ahmad ibn Ibrahim al-Ghazi, called the Gran (left-handed), who in the decades of the 1520s and 1530s caused the tide of battle to turn against the Ethiopians. The Christian dynasty had to flee its territory and much of Ethiopia was ravaged and occupied by the invading Muslims.

In the early sixteenth century the Portuguese had attempted, with little success, to establish relations with the Ethiopians. But the Muslim victories caused the harassed ruler Lebna Dengel (1508-40) to seek an alliance with the European Christians to help him regain possession of his kingdom. Despite considerable delay, the Portuguese did dispatch an expeditionary force of 400 men which arrived in

1541 during the reign of the ruler Galawdewos (1540-59). Armed with modern firearms, the Portuguese were commanded by Christovão da Gama, a son of the great discoverer. In 1543, after some difficult fighting, in which da Gama lost his life, the superior Portuguese military technology and discipline allowed a decisive triumph over the Muslims who had vainly secured armed Turks to aid their cause. Ahmad Gran was killed and the disorganized Muslim armies retreated permanently to their coastal homelands, leaving the Ethiopians once more in control of their territory.

The survivors of the Portuguese military remained in Ethiopia where they disappeared as a separate entity. The expedition, which undoubtedly had appeared at a critical moment in Ethiopian history, was basically the only Portuguese direct involvement in the African Christian state. Obviously the Portuguese government had determined that there was little profit or military support for their Indian Ocean empire to be gained from Ethiopia. If the Ethiopian ruler really was Prester John, he had proved himself too weak a sovereign to be of any use to the Portuguese in their ambitious but unfulfilled schemes for conquest along the Muslim coasts of the Red Sea. Following some unfortunate experiences with the excessively intolerant zeal of Roman Catholic missionaries in the seventeenth century, the Coptic Christian Ethiopians expelled them and subsequently lost significant contact with the European world, developing their destinies in isolation until the early years of the nineteenth century.

What then had been the results of this initial modern contact between Africa and Europe? In a positive sense, really very little. The Portuguese presence on the mainland north of the Congo River, where only the small colony of Guinea eventually remained under Portuguese rule, had been largely limited to individual traders and to a few important commercial garrisons. The latter were mostly permanently conquered by the Dutch during the period from 1580 to 1640 when the Portuguese nation was ruled by the Spanish king.[2] The traders remained, however, often marrying and being absorbed into African society. A variant of the Portuguese language consequently long survived as a means of commercial communication. But the numbers of Portuguese present had simply been too few to bring about many lasting changes during their relatively short period of occupation. The Portuguese impact upon the Kongo state, after its promising beginnings, had been to wreck its stability. The influences which remained were merely survivals of the initial period persisting in religion for example, in forms without any significant meaning for those following them. In Angola, which developed into a supplier of slaves for the New World, the Portuguese remained for many years essentially confined to a few coastal regions. From them a commercial network, maintained by Africans and the issue of Portuguese-African interbreeding, reached into a distant interior to draw slaves to the coastal markets. In Moçambique the Portuguese position was even more tenuous, limited to a few small ports, notably Moçambique island. The real upholders of the small Portuguese presence were individual landholders, the residents of *prazos* (a form of the *donatário* system), who were usually more African than Portuguese in origin, and who at best paid a nominal homage to the government in Lisbon. In

2. The Portuguese ruler Sebastian (1557-78) had lost his life in an ill-fated invasion of Morocco in 1578, thus allowing his state to pass in dynastic succession to the monarch of Spain.

neither of its future extensive colonies of Angola or Moçambique were there enough Portuguese settlers or missionaries to make any significant cultural impact on the large African populations. This situation of limited occupation lasted essentially until the quickening pace of European expansion into Africa during the latter part of the nineteenth century at last caused the Portuguese to revivify their dormant holdings to save them from passing entirely under the control of competing European rivals.

Europeans in West Africa

The subjects of other European nations had not delayed unduly in following the Portuguese to the newly discovered African coasts. An early rivalry with Spain was settled by the Treaty of Tordesillas of 1494 which divided the emerging regions of the hitherto unvisited parts of the world at a line drawn 370 leagues to the west of the Cape Verde Islands (at about approximately the forty-sixth parallel). Portugal received the territories to the east of the line, thus confirming possession of its African discoveries. The agreement was sanctified by various papal bulls. The Protestant sea powers of Britain and the Netherlands naturally did not accept the validity of this decision. Catholic France was no more satisfied; the sarcastic statement, "I would like to see Adam's will wherein he divided the earth between Spain and Portugal," was a reaction attributed to Francis I. A compliant pope later rectified the situation for France, thus allowing the French government to support, and to extend when policy dictated, what individual Frenchmen already were doing in Africa.

By the seventeenth century these several competing nations had established a series of limited holdings along the western African coast from the regions near the mouth of the Senegal River southward to Angola. France, which eventually established its early West African base in Senegal, drawn there by the false hope of an important navigable waterway leading into the interior, did not participate greatly in the search for new territories, in Africa or elsewhere, until the reign of Francis I (1515-47). Then the French, especially those directed by the merchant and government official, Jean Ango—whose approach to exploration was roughly parallel in method to that of Henry the Navigator—became active competitors in the world contest. The first important steps for the Senegal region came during Cardinal Richelieu's administration of French policy (1624-42) when trading companies, in which the state exercised predominant interest over a few reluctant private capitalists, initially were established. In 1638 a French *comptoir* was attempted near the mouth of the Senegal River; in 1659 the later principal French settlement of Saint Louis was founded. A main reason for the French concern to possess a West African base was the desire to find a secure source of slaves for the West Indian colonies of France, which in the mid-seventeenth century began to develop flourishing sugar plantations.

As part of his overall effort to make French administration more efficient, the mercantilist genius, Jean Baptiste Colbert, during his tenure of office (1661-83) at first resolved to follow the profitable examples offered by the British and Dutch East India companies. A French West Indies Company, which controlled the settlements in Senegal, was created in 1664; one of its objectives was to insure an adequate supply of slaves for the West Indian colonies. But France never realized much success in drawing slaves from this region of Africa. Consequently the French West Indies Company was replaced in 1672 by a new organization, the Senegal Company. Henceforth, even if sufficient numbers of slaves never were forthcoming from Senegal, forcing France's West Indian plantations to purchase their workers from other slave-supplying nations, the French nonetheless maintained a lasting colonial base despite the difficulties caused by hostilities stemming from European wars. Under the efficient leadership of André Bruë, governor of the settlement from 1697 to 1702, and from 1714 to 1720, some of the earliest European moves into the African interior, to a distance of about 500 miles, were undertaken in an effort to reach the regions which supplied gold for the western Sudan's North African trade. These endeavors were not overly successful, but the infant French colony found instead a profitable trade in gum, used for the printing of textiles and in the manufacture of medicines, to justify its continued development. African and French traders expanded this trade and the resulting prosperity of Saint Louis and other settlements allowed the flourishing of a lasting Afro-European cultural intermixture. By the end of the eighteenth century, Saint Louis, with a population of about 10,000 Africans and Europeans, was one of the major European establishments in Africa.

Along the Gold Coast during the seventeenth century an active competition for trade was participated in by a host of European rivals. By 1637, the Dutch wars against the Portuguese cost the latter most of their colony in Brazil. Consequently the Dutch, behaving consistently with the mercantilist philosophy of the era, sought bases in West Africa to serve as a supply source for slaves and also conquered the

Portuguese territories in Angola. The Dutch had established their first center along the Gold Coast in 1612; by 1642 all of the Portuguese forts were in the hands of the Dutch West Indies Company, an organization founded in 1621 hopefully to emulate the flourishing Dutch East India Company. The Dutch retained most of the conquered settlements, even though Brazil was retaken by the Portuguese and the Angolan settlements were seized by a Portuguese expedition sent from Brazil in 1648; they henceforth sold their African slaves to the labor-hungry Spanish and French colonies in the New World. By 1660 the British had officially entered the competition with the founding of their Company of Royal Adventurers Trading to Africa. This organization, with its African headquarters at Cape Coast, was granted a monopoly of trade from Gibraltar to the Cape of Good Hope, on the condition that it supply 3,000 slaves annually for the British West Indies. Any trader was free to participate in its ranks in return for the payment of a fee. The Royal Adventurers were succeeded in 1672 by the Royal Africa Company, an organization directed by an elected committee of merchants from the principal British ports of Bristol, London. and Liverpool. The company attempted to enforce a stricter monopoly since commercial interlopers had avoided the regulations of the previous company, but by 1698 their continuing competition had to be recognized by the opening of the right to trade to all who paid a fee. The Royal Africa Company also did not realize expected profits and it in turn was replaced in 1750 by the Company of Merchants Trading to Africa. This organization allowed all traders upon payment of a forty shilling fee to utilize its forts, for which it received an annual parliamentary maintenance grant. Other Europeans also opened forts along the Gold Coast at various times during the eighteenth century; they included the Swedes, Danes, and Brandenburgers. By the early eighteenth century there were about twenty-five major trading bases, plus as many minor ones. The British and the Dutch eventually emerged as the principal occupiers, although the Danes remained on the coast until 1850. As a result of the European wars of the eighteenth century the British gradually became the major commercial force along the 250-mile coastline.

Nevertheless, despite their many settlements, the Europeans remained largely subordinate to the wishes of the independent African political entities of the Gold Coast. The Africans held "notes" detailing the terms, including an annual payment, which the Europeans paid for the rights of occupation. And, since the commercial centers were occupied in an irregular sequence along the littoral by the outsiders, any difficulties caused by European intransigence led to the Africans diverting their trade to a more compliant rival. African military power also was a threat. In 1693, for example, the Akwamu state seized the Danish fort of Christianborg which they later sold back to its former possessors for a steep price. All of the Europeans and Africans present understood the local situation and generally acted to minimize conflict, and thus to maximize profits. European involvement in local affairs did not really occur until toward the end of the eighteenth century when the pressures generated by interior African states drew the resident foreigners into political life.

But even though the British, Dutch, and others were confined to their own settlements and had little interest in the cultural assimilation of Africans, some significant cultural intermingling did occur. African and Afro-European individuals rose to positions of influence in commerce, acquiring in various ways a knowledge of European procedures which allowed them to play an important role. And because a few Christian missionaries were sent to West Africa to handle the spiritual requirements of the resident Europeans, other Africans gained the opportunity for an extensive European education. They included, for example, Philip Quaque who was educated in Britain by the Society for the Propagation of the Gospel. Quaque was active as a minister and as a trader in the Gold Coast from his return in 1765 until his death in 1816, thus spreading the knowledge, both divine and secular, that he had acquired in Europe.

The few Africans educated in European fashion, however, were rare exceptions and their role must not be stressed unduly. Nevertheless, the small number of Africans significantly influenced by European culture made an important contribution to the small portion of Africa called the Gold Coast, giving it a lead in the formation of an indigenous Westernized elite. Armed with their knowledge of European ways, this continuing African elite later proved itself able to challenge their European rulers, in terms of the Europeans' own culture, at a far earlier period than was possible in most areas of Africa.

The overriding reason for the continued existence of most European settlements of all types along the western African coast eventually became their usefulness in successfully supplying sufficient numbers of unfortunate African victims for the trans-Atlantic slave trade. The Portuguese had seized Africans as early as the 1440s, bringing them back to labor in the underpopulated Portuguese homeland. The action was natural enough since slavery, both in Europe and Africa, was a recognized institution of that era. But this early manifestation of the slave trade by the Portuguese was a very limited one, even though the racist historian of southern Africa, George McCall Theal, postulated that the exportation of Africans to Portugal, where they were assimilated into the general population, was one reason for Portugal's decline from greatness![3]

The development of plantation economies in the Americas was required before the major drain of manpower from Africa began. The Portuguese, French, British, and others, especially from the seventeenth century, soon had created an ever-growing demand—since plantation slave populations normally did not reproduce themselves sufficiently to meet labor requirements—for laborers to work on their agricultural establishments cultivating sugar, tobacco, indigo, and other crops. Since slavery, usually in a mild form where slaves were recognized members of their particular African societies, was an integral part of the continent's life, Africans not unnaturally dealt more-or-less willingly with the early European traders seeking manpower. Most Africans, after all, had very little else to utilize in securing the European firearms, gunpowder, cloths, and sundry luxury items which increasingly became a desired goal of their commercial endeavors. But the traditional sources of slaves in African society were not able to satisfy the growing demand caused by the voracious plantation owners of the New World. Soon particular African states, either willingly or as a defensive measure, evolved into great slave-supplying nations through the results of successful aggression against their neighbors. African slavery also arose partly through the misuse by the ruling groups of their traditional forms of authority (as, for example, the punishment for crimes committed)

3. George McCall Theal, *The Portuguese in South Africa from 1505 to 1795* (London, 1927), p. 27.

which allowed slaves to be made from among their own subjects. The Ashanti peoples inland from the Fanti of the Gold Coast, the many small polities of the Niger delta region, and the Fon state of Dahomey were all outstanding examples of these forms of development.

In the past there has been much unfounded speculation about the numbers of Africans involved in the slave trade across the Atlantic Ocean to the New World, with some estimates running as high as over 100 million individuals. But the painstaking researches of a contemporary American scholar have recently provided us carefully derived base estimates for an evaluation of the trade. According to Philip D. Curtin, approximately 275,000 Africans had arrived in the Americas by 1600; 1,328,000 between 1600 and 1700; 6,265,000 between 1700 and 1810; and 1,628,000 from the latter date to 1870—in all making a total of 9,500,000. If an accepted figure of one-fifth is added to provide for the losses suffered during the traumatic passage across the Atlantic, a grand total of 11,360,000 Africans were removed from the continent.[4] These figures of course do not include the large numbers of Africans—which are impossible to estimate—who lost their lives in the wars devoted to slave raiding, or in the famines and other disorders which beset the survivors of the suffering societies. Nonetheless, without at all disregarding the undoubted horrors of every aspect of this inhumane trade, which ranks as one of the greatest examples of man's inhumanity to his fellow creatures, it must be pointed out that many African societies, or at least their ruling groups, benefited from the profits drawn from the trade.

4. Phillip D. Curtin, *The Atlantic Slave Trade* (Madison, 1969); J. D. Fage, *History of West Africa: An Introductory Survey,* 4th ed. (Cambridge, 1969). pp. 82-84.

And also the African regions hardest hit by the trade were then and remain yet among the most densely populated areas of the continent. Some observers have estimated that only about 1 percent per year of their population was lost to the trade. Nevertheless these unfortunate African captives were the youngest and most vigorous members of their societies who probably would have advanced their own civilization if they had been left to live out their lives in their homelands.

The Dutch in South Africa

At the Southern tip of the African continent a very different variation of the encounter between Africans and Europeans had been evolving since the middle of the seventeenth century. European interest had come late to this region because of the relatively barren environment of its coast and the reputed hostility of its pastoral Khoikhoi inhabitants—the Dutch derogatively called them Hottentots—who lived thinly scattered along the western and southern coasts. The Khoikhoi ranged in individual clan organizations numbering in the hundreds, a grouping of which made up an independent, loosely structured political entity which could include thousands of individuals. By the mid-seventeenth century, in the area south of the Orange River, the Khoikhoi probably had a population of about 200,000. The ravages of European-introduced diseases, plus the policies of the Dutch invaders, reduced this number to about 20,000 by 1800. One early example of the supposed Khoikhoi attitude to outsiders had been the hostilities which caused the death of the great Portuguese Indian Ocean commander, Francisco da Almeida, which occurred in 1510 when he landed searching for provisions on his return voyage to his homeland. But although the Portuguese subsequently were not interested in a settlement, the increasing number of voyages to the east by the Dutch, after the successful foundation of their empire in the East Indies, led them to the search for a suitable location providing a safe harbor capable of supplying provisions for the long journey. The harbor of modern Cape Town possessed a satisfactory fresh water source and thus in 1652 Jan van Riebeeck and a few followers landed with orders to create a way station, under the jurisdiction of the East India Company's government at Batavia, for Dutch vessels.

The great distances involved, however, insured that the settlers at the Cape had much local autonomy. Despite reiterated orders stressing that the newcomers should remain at peace with their African neighbors, it proved impossible to prevent friction between the various independent groups of Khoikhoi and the Dutch. Hostilities began as early as 1653. Initially the Dutch rulers had not planned on developing a colony of settlers, but the need for increasing amounts of provisions for the steady flow of vessels to the east led to the dispatch of additional European reinforcements before the end of the 1650s. Friction between the settlers and their distant superiors began almost immediately when the colonists reacted against the prices for their crops fixed by the governors of the East India Company. Despite the difficulties, however, when van Riebeeck left after completing a ten-year tour of duty, the population had reached almost 1,400, including slaves drawn from Java, Madagascar, and Angola. Out of the varied European and slave groups, plus the remnants of Khoikhoi, came the ancestors of the Cape Colored populations.

The colonists increasingly disregarded the desires of their government that they concentrate their energies upon ill-compensated agricultural pursuits, instead turning their energies to cattle and sheep herding. The Dutch administration had little alternative but to realistically accept and then to try to regulate this evolution. Additional settlers came in the 1680s when French Huguenots, fleeing religious persecution in their homeland, emigrated to South Africa. The French government consistently retarded its own colonial development, in Africa and elsewhere, by allowing only Roman Catholics to people its overseas settlements. Conscious government policy soon integrated the French Protestants with the Dutch colonists, and with other Dutch and German arrivals the initial basic European immigration to the Cape was ended by the first two decades of the eighteenth century.

Their increasing numbers caused the Europeans to continuously move inland as *trekboers*, pastoralists moving about with their herds. The Khoikhoi were decimated quickly by war and by disease, especially smallpox. The other indigenous Africans residing inland from the Cape, the San (or Bushmen), a purely hunting and gathering society living in small, independent bands of from 50 to 100 individuals, similarly suffered. Wars of extermination, in fact, were waged upon the San by the Dutch, since the hunters continually preyed upon the settlers' cattle. By the 1770s the Europeans also encountered near the Great Fish River, the advancing tide of Bantu-speakers. Both Dutch and Bantu were cattle-keeping peoples and endemic hostilities soon were underway.

The colony's economic problems continued, with its expenses consistently outrunning its revenues. One result was an increase in the use of slave labor, although the nature of the environment precluded any extensive New World-type plantation economy based on African and East Indian captives. By the 1770s the Dutch empire was in general decline, a fate shared by the East India Company, which paid its last dividend in 1782. Dutch weakness drew other Europeans to attempt the securing of control over the Cape's strategic location upon the sea route to the east. The French occupied the Cape from 1781 to 1784 during the worldwide hostilities stemming from the American Revolution. When they left, the colony continued along its unprofitable way, with the East India Company becoming bankrupt in 1794. Beset by frontier wars with the Bantu, especially the loosely organized Xhosa, as well as by unruly settlers striking out against their inefficient government, the Dutch colony easily fell to the British during the wars of the French Revolution and the Napoleonic era. They occupied the Cape from 1795 to 1803, and again from 1806 to 1815, when the British insisted upon possession of the territory from the peace settlement ending the Napoleonic wars.

Nevertheless by the close of the eighteenth century the European population in the southernmost section of the continent, despite its internal weakness, was the only sizeable body of its kind in Africa. With over 20,000 colonists, supported by more than 25,000 slaves, the Dutch far outnumbered the next largest European settlement, that of the French in Senegal. But the Dutch influence was of an unusual nature, their culture outside of Cape Town (then possessing about 15,000 African and European inhabitants) being largely shaped by the African environments in which they lived and by the narrow Calvinistic faith which shaped their thoughts. The latter entrenched the settlers in a predestined position of superiority over the "inferior" African peoples, which they dominated by means of their superior technology and military organization. In the remainder of the continent, apart from the limited groups of Africans sharing influences with the British, French, Dutch, Portuguese, Spaniards, or Danes in their various settlements, the impact of Europe was extremely limited. The vast interior of Africa remained virtually unknown to the Europeans clustered along Africa's coasts, scarcely in fact better known than in the distant era of Roman rule in North Africa. Beginning ventures were underway, however, by individual European explorers, such as James Bruce in the Sudan and Ethiopia and Mungo Park in western Africa, to set the stage for the major task of opening Africa to the outside world which was to be accomplished by the Europeans of the nineteenth century.

3   Europe Conquers Africa

In the last quarter of the eighteenth century several developing currents of European endeavor emerged to fundamentally alter the balance of relationships hitherto evolved between Africa and Europe. They included the humanitarian reaction to the inhuman excesses of slavery and the slave trade; the beginnings of a new European territorial expansion into Africa, as well as the extension of the previously existing contacts; the awakening stimulus within Christianity which led to an interest in the evangelizing of non-Europeans; and, perhaps most important, the burst of energy devoted to the filling of the gaps in all branches of contemporary knowledge.

55

The Campaign against the Slave Trade

There had always been a vocal minority of humane Europeans appalled by the cruelties of slavery and the trade in slaves. They ranged from the obscure German Mennonites of Germantown, Pennsylvania, who spoke out against the slave trade and slavery in 1688, to the famous author of *De l'esprit des lois,* Baron de Montesquieu. And, for example, in the latter's homeland, it was ruled as early as 1607 that any baptized person entering France was automatically free. But the leaders of the French society and government of the end of the eighteenth century were too involved at first in the all-consuming task of reforming French internal institutions to give much effective attention to the excesses connected with the institution of slavery, particulary when France's most profitable colonies, especially Saint Domingue (present-day Haiti), based their considerable wealth upon that institution. Thus despite the efforts of the French Société des Amis des Noirs (founded in 1788), the effective movement to abolish the evils of slavery and the slave trade rather began in Britain, the ruler of Europe's major overseas slave-holding empire.

The first active steps of the abolitionists within Britain were directed to the amelioration of the conditions of life of a large class of poor blacks, often abandoned by their callous masters, which had considerable difficulties in surviving the unfamiliar environment of the British Isles. One individual devoted to the cause of alleviating human suffering, Granville Sharp, undertook the care of an ill slave, Josiah Strong, abandoned without care by his owner. When Strong's health improved, and consequently his value returned, his owner attempted to repossess him. Sharp fought the case in the courts, but in the end it was dropped. Sharp nevertheless continued his campaign, and in the case of another slave, James Somerset, Chief Justice Lord Mansfield in 1772 announced his famous decision that slavery was not recognized by the laws of Britain—the ruling did not, however, affect colonial territories. Many owners therefore ceased caring for their former slaves, from whom no profit was any longer to be gained, and the black poor population of Britain grew significantly. About 15,000 slaves were freed by the decision.

To meet this problem Sharp and other reformers advocated a scheme, which was partially supported by the British government, for returning the distressed blacks to Africa. There it was hoped that they might lead a better life, while at the same time, according to the designs of the reformers, serving as a model for the future Christian regeneration of their continent. The first settlers, over 400 Africans and Europeans, arrived in 1787 in what became the West African colony of Sierra Leone. The difficulties of establishing a settlement in a hostile environment among the Temne people, led to the failure of the venture by 1790, but the British managers of the experiment persevered in their determination. A Sierra Leone Company was organized in 1791 to undertake a renewed effort, its endeavors culminating with the foundation of a settlement at Freetown. Included in the new body of settlers in Sierra Leone were 1,200 former slaves of the newly independent American colonists; they had joined the British forces during the Revolution on the promise of their freedom. But subsequently they had not been well treated, having been sent to the harsh climate of Nova Scotia where, in addition, the pledges that they would receive adequate land had not been fully honored. Later arrivals to the struggling colony were, through agreement with the British who wished to remove their unsettling presence, fugitive slaves from Jamaica, the Maroons.

It was a difficult experiment for those Africans and descendants of Africans. Lacking adequate capital resources of their own, they had to follow the directions of a not always efficient or sympathetic philanthropic company. Disease also took a heavy toll among black as well as white. And the settlers faced hostility from the indigenous Africans who could not regard with favor this creation of a growing, land-hungry, settlement in their midst. Nonetheless the colonists did maintain their position until support was forthcoming from the British government. The Sierra Leone Company, ever in need of funds, received a royal charter and an annual subsidy from its government in 1800. When Great Britain abolished the slave trade throughout its empire in 1808, Sierra Leone became a crown colony designed to serve as a naval base for actions against slavers and as a depot for the settlement of liberated slaves. The experiment had succeeded, and in the future a stream of western-educated Africans, from the missionary-run schools of Sierra Leone, had an increasingly important impact in the several developing colonies of the British in West Africa.

Meantime the frontal assault to have the British slave trade ruled illegal was underway in Parliament. In 1783 a group of Quakers had appointed a committee to organize a permanent lobby to this end. Led by men of religious and humanitarian persuasions, such as William Wilberforce in Parliament and Thomas Clarkson as the indefatigable researcher furnishing telling information to support the spokesmen's arguments, the reformers evolved into one of Britain's most successful pressure groups. After many setbacks they triumphed with the passage of an act making British involvement in the slave trade illegal from January 1, 1808. Their success was a natural culmination of the changing intellectual climate of the eighteenth century which increasingly condemned the inhuman excesses of slavery and the slave trade. The task of the reformers was eased by changes in the nature of the economic structure of the British Empire. One class of influential slave owners had been removed from the contest through the American triumph of 1783, while in the British West Indies the decreasing fertility of the sugar-producing land, plus the adverse effects to the islands' commerce caused by the American Revolution and the Anglo-French wars, hindered the effectiveness of that important faction supporting the trade in slaves. These changes in economic patterns converged with the efficient zeal of the humanitarians to allow the passage of the law of March 1807 abolishing the slave trade.

The legislation of course required enforcement. Penalties were stringent—including a fine of £100 for every slave carried, plus the confiscation of the vessel and its entire cargo—and were made more so during the next two decades. Their efficient enforcement by the Royal Navy soon virtually ended the direct participation of British subjects in the outlawed commerce. The role of the Sierra Leone settlement has previously been mentioned. Britain, however, could not rest content, if it really wanted to end the slave trade, with the terms of an act which bound only British subjects. Without additional action the profitable trade merely would have passed to other carriers. Denmark had legislated to end the trade in 1804, the United States in 1808, Sweden in 1813, the

Netherlands in 1814, and the French, bowing to British pressure, in 1818, but few other nations had demonstrated much concern. France, during the heady days of the First Republic, had in 1794 not only abolished the trade, but also the institution of slavery as well. But the reaction following Napoleon's rise to power had negated this moral triumph, with both slavery and the trade in slaves being restored to their former legality in 1802.

Thus to carry forward the aims of British policy a series of agreements involving financial compensation, were negotiated with minor powers, such as Spain in 1817, and Portugal in 1815 and 1817. These agreements allowed the British to help enforce actions against the trade, although the continuing efforts of these nations to avoid enforcement required later additional action. Brazil, after gaining its independence, agreed to end the trade in 1831. But the major sea carriers of slaves, the French and the Americans, generally refused to allow the British to police their vessels for them. Both nations had, in their view, suffered enough in recent conflicts from the exercise of British predominance upon the seas to cause them to balk at any such proposal, no matter how compellingly the humanitarian aspect was stressed. The French and the Americans did initiate minor efforts to supervise the vessels of their nationals, and they at times did cooperate somewhat with the British, but until the years after the middle of the nineteenth century the chief labor of ending the trade to the New World remained with the British. Rival nations constantly accused Britain of seeking to gain political and economic advantage by its antislave trade activity, and of course the British did—as at Lagos on the Nigerian coast. Nevertheless the way was open for the critics to act if they had so decided. In this instance the spoils belonged to the virtuous.

A few individual Africans, some of whom had once been slaves, had participated in the movement to end the overseas slave trade. In Saint Domingue during the 1790s Africans and the descendants of Africans had by successful revolution ended the status of slavery itself. But the African polities sharing with European participants in the profits of slaving were not a consenting party to the European-made decision to end the commerce in slaves. Consequently Africans were forced to react to the hard economic reality that what had been a lucrative and legal commerce before the British reformers' victory in 1807 had become henceforth a morally reprehensible and illegal practice. And even though the decisions of the British Parliament had no legal value in African territory, the Royal Navy stood off the African rulers' coasts prepared to enforce the new legislation. There were naturally never enough British vessels available to police every suspected slaving port—in the 1840s there were only twenty vessels in service along the entire West African coast—and thus a clandestine trade continued. Nevertheless the ever-present danger of apprehension and possible bombardment remained an effective threat.

Other products had to be developed to replace the illegal slaves. In time, although the changeover was slow in many regions, the palm oil of the Niger Delta and other areas, and the peanuts of the Senegal region, both of which provided oil for lighting, the manufacture of soap, cooking, and for lubricating machines, became the most important western African substitutes, restoring the commercial prosperity lost to Africans by the cessation of the former trade. An enterprizing state like Dahomey, for example, even attempted, during the reign of its ruler Glele (1858-89), to blend both systems by putting its slaves to work in its own palm oil plantations. By the 1870s Dahomey was exporting annually palm oil worth £500,000. The ramifications of the post-slave trade economy for Africans were many, and they will be discussed below in their relationship to the other factors connected with the increasing European presence in nineteenth-century Africa.

France and Egypt

Europeans had been acquiring African territory since the Portuguese conquests beginning in the fifteenth century, although the pace of their expansion had remained slow until the nineteenth century. But that century began with Napoleon Bonaparte's invading army holding Egypt following the easy French victory at the Battle of the Pyramids (1798) over the Mamluk vassals of the Ottoman Turkish sultan who had ruled Egypt since 1517. Napoleon's schemes for Egypt, a part of his strategy designed to threaten the vital British position in India, included a thoroughgoing reform of its corrupt administration, a process which he claimed would allow the indigenous Muslim inhabitants a large role in their own governance. Included in Napoleon's retinue was a large group of scholars who during the brief French occupation founded the modern study of ancient Egypt. Their discoveries included the finding of the Rosetta Stone, which led to the translation of the ancient Egyptian hieroglyphics. British naval supremacy, however, made clear by Horatio Nelson's victory over Napoleon's fleet at Abukir Bay and by the subsequent British support for the Ottoman enemies of the French in Syria, ended the French leader's grandiose plans. The future French emperor hurried back to his homeland, leaving the French army to hold on in Egypt without outside support. A British-led expedition ended the French occupation in 1801. With no interest then in occupying the Ottoman Empire's Egyptian province, the British evacuated their military forces, leaving the country in considerable disorder.

Out of the confused flux of the postwar situation rose a Turkish army officer, Muhammad Ali; he founded a dynasty which directed Egypt until its financial excesses finally led to British military intervention in the 1880s. Though the French occupation had been a very transitory one, it nonetheless had had a lasting impact upon Egyptian society. With the outmoded system of Ottoman rule shattered, the dynamic and talented Muhammad Ali, who ruled from 1805 to 1848, strove with considerable success to modernize Egypt, relying extensively upon European (especially French) support in the educational, technical, economic, and military spheres. The effort was the beginning of a process which ultimately occurred in each future independent African state. Their occupation also influenced the French military, since this first French extensive contact with a Muslim population had its impact in the attitudes which their conquering forces brought after 1830 to Algeria.

Britain and South Africa

At the other end of the continent the British, because of the circumstances of the wars of the French Revolutionary and Napoleonic eras, did become involved in the early partition of Africa. The weak Dutch position centered at the Cape of Good Hope, located on the vital route to the British Indian empire, invited intervention, as the brief French occupation of the early 1780s had demonstrated. Thus when a European peace settlement finally came in 1814 the South African Dutch colony was one of the few African and Asian territories retained by the British. Once occupying South Africa, however, the new rulers found themselves as unable as the Dutch before them to control effectively the outlying regions where Afrikaners and Africans met. The British were continuously involved in hostilities and border tensions which had to be dealt with and paid for by their government. The introduction of elements of British custom and law to South Africa, designed to control the unruly Afrikaner inhabitants who had previously been growing exceedingly restive even under the inefficient Dutch administration, caused much additional unrest. Especially hated by the Afrikaners were regulations concerning the treatment of slaves and dependent Africans. The Fiftieth Ordinance of 1828, for example, was designed to improve the lot of the Khoikhoi and other Africans employed by the white community. In 1834, following the triumph of the British abolitionists in Parliament during the previous year in legislating the end of slavery in the British Empire, that institution was legally ended in South Africa.

One principal Afrikaner reaction to the many changes brought by the British administration was the Great Trek, beginning in 1835, an organized movement of Afrikaners which culminated a continuing tendency on their part to move ever farther into the interior in an effort to escape the influences of the government ruling in Cape Town. The growing population of the Afrikaner inhabitants seeking land, which had become increasingly limited in the older settled regions, was also a primary reason for the migration. By 1845 about 14,000 migrants—men, women, and children—had crossed the Orange River. The exodus, at first left unregulated by the British who could take few inexpensive measures to stop the troublesome Afrikaners from departing, led to the founding of settlements in the future South African provinces of Natal, the Orange Free State, and the South African Republic (the Transvaal). But the relations of the Afrikaners with the surrounding hostile African populations in the territories beyond the British jurisdiction caused reactions which endangered, from the British point of view, their hold of the strategic Cape. Consequently in 1843 a first major step was taken in Natal: that region was annexed by Britain to ensure that the Afrikaners did not control a position along the seacoast potentially dangerous to British interests. In 1848 the British extended their inland frontier beyond the Orange River. After other difficulties with the Afrikaners in the interior the British, by the Sand River Convention of 1852 with the Transvaal and the Bloemfontein Convention of 1854 with the Orange Free State, abandoned their responsiblities for regulating the continuing crises between African and Afrikaner. But this solution, which recognized the independence of the Afrikaner republics, was not practicable because of the endemic unrest with Africans stimulated by the Afrikaner states. The continuing disorder forced the British to retake the initiative. They annexed in 1868 the Basuto state of the charismatic ruler Moshesh to save it from conquest by the Orange Free State. And with the continuation of the problems caused by the independent Afrikaners additional British intervention would be required in the future.

France in Senegal and Algeria

During the first half of the nineteenth century the French were especially active in two areas of Africa, Senegal and Algeria. Their presence in Senegal dated from the mid-seventeenth century, but despite the measures attempted for inland expansion during the administration of André Bruë, and the renewed efforts under Pierre-Félix David from 1738 to 1746, French holdings remained essentially limited to the coast. After reoccupying Senegal, which had been seized by the British during the Napoleonic wars, the French attempted in 1817 a scheme for the development of a plantation economy growing cotton and indigo. Based upon the profitable Dutch model of their East Indies colony, the venture was under the direction of Julien Schmaltz, who had experience in the East, and later under Baron Roger, governor of Senegal from 1822 to 1827. Faced by the indifference and hostility of the indigenous Africans, to whom the new system necessarily looked much like forced labor or slavery, and of problems for the growth of the new crops in the Senegalese environment, the scheme faded away during the 1820s without lasting result. Senegal returned to the long-established gum trade for its economic life, in which the principal commercial roles were undertaken by Afro-Europeans and Africans. Beginning in the 1830s the Africans began to cultivate peanuts which eventually became the mainstay of the colony's development.

Nevertheless, despite the uncertain economic development of Senegal, a significant blending of African and European cultures and populations occurred over the years at the commercial centers of Saint Louis and Gorée. The former city included at the end of the eighteenth century about 600 Europeans among its approximately 10,000 inhabitants, the largest number present in any West African European settlement. Also included in the population were many Afro-Europeans. They and the free Africans, locally known as *habitants*, had become assimilated in varying degrees to French ways. In 1833 the French government declared that any free individuals in their colonies were eligible to receive French citizenship; little action was taken, however, to make the decree a reality. But during the 1840s the inhabitants of Senegal profited from the changes occurring within metropolitan France to gain special political rights which set them off from all other contemporary Africans subject to European rule. This tendency culminated in 1848 when France abolished slavery in its colonies and awarded the status of equal citizenship to the inhabitants of its empire, including about 12,000 mostly illiterate and non-Christian Africans of Senegal. The 1848 decree also allowed the new French citizens to continue to be ruled in matters of land ownership, inheritance, marriage, and divorce by their own traditional law. As a result of the political changes a Senegalese-born Afro-European, Durand Valentin, was elected in 1848 to represent Senegal in the French legislature. This important exception to the usual method of administrating African colonies was not extended to other territories, even in Senegal, when the French later began their major expansion in the continent. Other dynamic colonial policies for Senegal waited the term of the driving French governor, Louis Faidherbe, during the 1850s and the 1860s.

While this exceptional cultural intermingling went forward in Senegal, the French became involved in a major colonial venture in Algeria. Since the sixteenth century, when the famous Mediterranean sea raiders Aruj and Khayr al-Din had answered a call from the citizens of Algiers to expel Spanish invaders from a strategic island dominating that port's harbor, Algiers and its indefinite hinterland had been a nominal part of the Ottoman Turkish Empire. The effective direction of affairs within Algiers, however, had soon passed to the janissaries, resident Turkish troops, who through continuous recruiting in their homeland, formed a permanent ruling elite. The Turkish Sublime Porte accepted this situation as long as its suzerainty was recognized and at least some tribute was paid. Eventually the ruling class became represented by one official, the Dey of Algiers, an individual who was replaced frequently by his violent comrades. There were, for example, twenty-eight deys between 1671 and 1830. The indigenous populations of the Turkish dependency normally had no role in the direction of affairs.

During the French Revolutionary and Napoleonic wars Algiers had furnished much-needed grain supplies to the embattled French government, but in the years after 1815 entangled questions over payment embittered relations between the two states. Finally, in 1827, a most undipolmatic French agent, Pierre Deval, so angered Dey Husayn that the Muslim ruler lost his temper, swatting the Frenchman with his fly switch. The French government interpreted this blow as an insult to their state and instituted a blockade of Algiers to compel its government to give redress. The show of French force, however, had little harmful effect upon the Algerian state, with affairs remaining at a stalemate until the government of Charles X, searching for a measure to increase the popularity of its flagging regime, decided to invade the nominally Ottoman territory in 1830.

The rulers of Algiers, who had been threatened with little result by various European powers during the centuries of Turkish domination, did not undertake serious preparations to resist the French. Because of this misplaced confidence the Dey's forces were easily defeated in 1830 despite a generally mismanaged landing by the French military. Husayn was forced to conclude a peace agreement which provided for his exile from Algiers, leaving the French with the task of deciding exactly what they should do with the new conquest. The victory had brought no benefit to the government of Charles X, which fell in the July Revolution of 1830, and the succeeding regime of Louis Philippe was handed the task of deciding France's future—if any—in North Africa.

While an uncertain France delayed a decision about Algeria's future, the military had to begin a colonial policy to maintain order in the conquered territory, an undertaking complicated by the presence of French and other private individuals who had not delayed in following French troops across the Mediterranean. These individuals supplied the military with essential services and, more important for the future, took advantage of the chaotic conditions in an Algeria deprived of its traditional governing class to oppress the indigenous population. While such unfair practices went on, France finally came to a decision concerning Algeria. A legislative commission reported in 1834 that the conquered territory—only a very limited part of present Algeria—should remain a French possession. It was to be administered by the military under the supervision of the Ministry of War.

But the French government quickly learned, as had British administrators in India and South Africa, that the originally planned policy of a limited territorial occupation in Algeria was not a realistic approach for a country without fixed boundaries that was inhabited by unstable political groupings. The military leaders in the colony were tempted continually to expand the area under domination in the usually vain hope of attaining full security for the already conquered lands. By 1837, after a previous significant failure before its fortifications, the French seized Constantine, the key city of Algeria's eastern coastal region. In addition, the French had earlier begun pushing towards Oran, the city holding a similar position to the west of Algiers. During the latter campaign they encountered one of the most tenacious and imaginative of all the Algerian leaders who attempted to halt the French conquest. Abd al-Qadir, the twenty-four-year-old son of a Muslim holy man, and a religious personage in his own right—he had visited Arabia—in 1832 took the lead of a confederation of tribesmen centered near Oran. While on his travels to the east Abd al-Qadir had observed the modernizing reforms of Muhammad Ali of Egypt; he now attempted to follow roughly similar policies for his own incipient polity. Especially noteworthy were the Arab leader's efforts to organize a well-trained army equipped with modern weapons—he had some European officers to aid in this development—and to create a stable administration capable of supplying regular financial resources. Though all the indigenous Algerians of the western region did not follow his lead, Abd al-Qadir achieved enough success in creating a powerful following that in 1834 a French officer concluded a treaty with him recognizing the Arab chieftain as the ruler of the territory around Oran. The Frenchman had clearly thought it preferable to attempt to work with the local leader to achieve order rather than to fight against him. A later agreement at Tafna in 1837 extended Abd al-Qadir's authority. Both French negotiators of these accords had gone beyond the expressed orders of their government, but once they were signed it was thought best by the directors of French policy to let them stand. But by this time Abd al-Qadir's position had been considerably strengthened and in his mind the treaties opened the way for a further expansion of his influence within Algeria, especially toward the east.

Meanwhile inceasing numbers of European settlers had been entering Algeria to profit from the policies of an administration little concerned with rendering justice to the conquered Muslims. By 1840, for example, there were about 30,000 European civilians in the territory, most of them living in urban areas, but with an important minority numbering about 2,500 resident in the countryside. This unorganized pattern of settlement was underway despite the fact that the limited number of French troops stationed in Algeria was unable to give the isolated rural newcomers adequate protection. The unregulated expansion came to a quick end in 1839 when Abd al-Qadir, following friction with the French over the extent of his jurisdiction, launched his army against the wedge of colonists extending inland from Algiers. The settlements were destroyed without difficulty, while the French army, lacking leaders able to come to terms with an enemy utilizing its own countryside to full advantage, lost the military initiative to its Muslim opponents.

The situation was saved for France with the appointment in 1840 of General Thomas-Robert Bugeaud as military commander in Algeria. A hardbitten veteran of the Napoleonic wars, where he had worked his way to command from the ranks, Bugeaud, through his experiences in the bitterly fought Spanish campaign, was cognizant of the need to adapt tactics to local circumstances. Once arrived in Algeria the new commander pushed a reluctant military to reform its organization, abandoning its dependence upon stationary garrisons, which were supplied with difficulty by heavily laden relief expeditions, creating mobile columns of about 7,000 men to seek out and destroy Abd al-Qadir's followers. The French government also provided increased military support; by 1846, 108,000 troops, constituting one-third of the total French army, were engaged in Algeria. Bugeaud realized that, once in battle, the superior French firepower and discipline normally would insure victory. And to insure that his Muslim enemies received minimal support from their coreligionists of the settled population, Bugeaud adopted a scorched-earth policy against any regions found in any way supporting Abd al-Qadir. The tactics worked. Defeated in battle by 1843, Abd al-Qadir was forced onto the defensive. An attempt by the Algerian leader to gain support from the ruler of Morocco, Mawlay Abd al-Rahman, which had some initial success, ended when Bugeaud defeated the Moroccans at Isly in 1844. The French also bombarded the Moroccan ports of Tangier and Mogador. Fearing the consequences of further conflict, the Moroccan sultan left Abd al-Qadir to his fate. He finally surrendered to the French in December 1847. Eventually sent to an exile in Damascus, the Algerian resistance leader remained there until his death in 1883.

Bugeaud was more than an efficient and charismatic military leader; he also utilized his dominating position within the colony to set the pattern for other developments in French Algeria. The folly of the policy of unregulated European settlement had been made all too apparent by the tactics of Abd al-Qadir. To avoid future tragedies for colonists,

Bugeaud undertook to inaugurate a careful policy of government-regulated expansion, utilizing the army to prepare designated settlement sites for newcomers. The soldiers themselves also were encouraged to participate: veterans were given liberal land grants to induce residence in Algeria once their term of military service was completed. (In this policy Bugeaud was reviving a technique used during the Roman times in North Africa.) This organized approach to peopling the territory with Europeans was successful. By the time that Bugeaud left Algeria in 1847 the number of European residents had risen to 109,400, with 15,000 of them living in rural areas. Despite succeeding military and economic crises in the period before the 1880s, the European population steadily continued to grow, much aided by a healthy birthrate. By 1881 the colonists numbered 376,000.

The resulting European population of Algeria had some similarities with that of the Afrikaner settlers of South Africa. It had become an indigenous population, knowing no other homeland but Africa, always tenaciously ready to defend its privileged position against the surrounding African masses. Both European groups were willing to exploit the subordinate Africans with as much brutality as their respective metropolitian governments allowed. But there were significant differences between the settlers of North and South Africa. The emerging Afrikaner people of the south, an amalgam of Dutch, French, German, and other stock, were faced during the nineteenth century with an offsetting population of British derivation settled there through governmental initiative. The newcomers naturally tended to dominate many facets of colonial life, particularly in the areas nearest the coast. And the British colonial system, with its emphasis upon the gradual evolution of local self-government by European residents—responsible government came to Cape Colony, for example, in 1853, and internal self-government in 1872—was foreign to the French system.

Algeria attracted many non-French immigrants, notably from Spain: in 1846, 62,106 of the total population of 109,400 were foreigners. But eventually a standardized French educational system for Europeans ensured that those individuals born in Algeria became French. In addition, the closeness of Algeria to France, joined to the underlying administrative assimilative tendencies of the French governmental system caused the overseas French to seek legislative absorbtion into the metropolitan structure. This goal was achieved initially following the 1848 revolution in France when the three Algerian provinces centered around the cities of Algiers, Oran, and Constantine were incorporated as French departments. All sent representatives to the French legislature. The administration of Napoleon III ended elective representation for the French of Algeria in 1852, yet the ideal remained as an objective of settler policy. There were several changes in administrative forms for Algeria in the period before the 1870s, although whatever the system the Algerian French made their views heard in France. Because their cooperation was needed to keep the Algerian Muslims at peace, settler opinions were heeded to insure the continuance of their dominating position within Algeria.

In other regions of Africa, before the 1880s, the European presence was not as noticeable as in South Africa, Algeria, or even Senegal, but there was nonetheless considerable European influence in many coastal areas. The British maintained their freed-slave colony of Sierra Leone and a small settlement in Gambia, plus their forts along the Gold Coast. The

Dutch continued the occupation of their Gold Coast trading settlements until 1872 when they transferred their holdings to the British. To the south the British, after a decade of intervention, annexed Lagos in 1861 in a measure connected with their policies against the slave trade. The French maintained a few establishments along the littoral between Senegal and the Gold Coast, and from 1849 farther south in Gabon they developed Libreville as a paler imitation of Freetown. None of these French settlements were very important. The Portuguese continued, as indicated earlier, to hold on to their possessions in Angola and Moçambique. In East Africa north of Moçambique there were no official European settlements. An Arab-dominated state based upon the island of Zanzibar exercised varying influence over African peoples along the coast and into the interior. Through Zanzibar's sultan the British maintained a predominant influence over all European rivals, gaining this position by upholding Zanzibar's rulers against rivals in return for Zanzibari assistance in British initiatives designed to end the trade in slaves from eastern Africa to Arabia and the regions bordering the Persian Gulf. France did possess minor colonial settlements on Mayotte, in the Comoro Islands, and on the island of Nosy Bé off the northwestern coast of Madagascar, but they were of little significance. The great island of Madagascar remained free of European control, although British and French missionaries and traders at times held considerable influence.

Exploring Africa: The Niger

If the interior of the vast continent, apart from the twin points of continuous penetration in Algeria and South Africa, remained free of European influence, developments were underway in the long-delayed exploration of Africa which were of great consequence for the future. The many individual ventures into the African interior are too numerous to discuss here, but selected examples will illustrate the manner in which exploration, through the often outstanding feats of resolute men, brought Africa and Africans to the attention of the European public.

The solution of the problem of the unknown course and outlet of the Niger River was one of the first quests to draw European interest. Rising in the hills of the Futa Jalon, in modern Guinea, and then flowing 1,000 miles to the northeast, the great river turned southeast near Timbuktu, flowing on until it disappeared into the delta region of the Nigerian coast, thus passing unnoticed into the Atlantic Ocean. The lack of knowledge concerning the important African waterway drew the attention of a newly organized British organization, the Assocation for Promoting the Discovery of the Interior Parts of Africa—called the African Association—which had been formed in 1788 for reasons of scientific curiosity, but also with the hopes that any discoveries it helped to accomplish could be utilized for the commercial benefit of Britain. After several unsuccessful efforts undertaken from North and West Africa, the association dispatched a young Scots doctor, Mungo Park, to West Africa in 1795. Heading inland from the Gambia, Park reached the Niger near Segu in 1796 and, although he was prevented from proceeding farther, the Scotsman did see that the river flowed from west to east, thus solving one of the mysteries of the Niger's course. With support from the Colonial Office, and accompanied by thirty-nine other Europeans, Mungo Park returned to Africa in 1805 to attempt to explore the river's course as far as possible while reporting upon its commercial potentiality. The European expedition was decimated by disease. Only five of its members, including Park, were able to make a final descent of the river. The survivors drowned in the Bussa rapids, about 800 miles down the river from Timbuktu, in 1806.

In 1822 the British government again supported the continuation of the quest by dispatching Walter Oudney, Dixon Denham, and Hugh Clapperton upon an expedition heading south from the North African port of Tripoli. Although Oudney died, Clapperton, while Denham was exploring elsewhere, successfully reached the important Hausa cities of Kano and Sokoto in Northern Nigeria where, although he gained much valuable information, he and Denham were blocked from following the Niger's course to the sea. Nevertheless they had ascertained that the Niger flowed to the south, and thus assuredly entered the Atlantic along the Nigerian coast. On a new expedition Clapperton again returned to solve the problem of the river, and also to conclude a convention against the slave trade with the Muslim ruler of Sokoto. He left Badagri, on the Nigerian coast, in 1825, accompanied among others by a resolute servant, Richard Lander. But Clapperton failed to sign the proposed convention, dying at Sokoto in 1826. However in 1830 Richard Lander, accompanied by his brother John, was sent inland by the Colonial Office, this time successfully proceeding down the Niger in a most difficult voyage, from the Bussa rapids to the Atlantic.

The major geographical question had finally been resolved, and a great African waterway was thus potentially open to those Europeans who were prepared to attempt to utilize it for the penetration of European commerce and

Christianity into the African interior. However European health problems blocked effective utilization until an expedition of 1854, led by W. B. Baikie, proved the usefulness of quinine against malaria. Previously an 1832-34 commercial expedition backed by the Liverpool merchant Macgregor Laird had lost about two-thirds of its members, while a government venture of 1841-42 suffered similar heavy losses.

Exploring Africa: The Nile and the Congo

While the Niger problem was being slowly resolved, European geographical attention turned to the question of the sources of another great African river, the Nile, an issue which had interested geographers from the days of Herodotus and Ptolemy. The Blue Nile, the main supplier of water for the Nile's annual flooding in Egypt, had its Ethiopian source discovered by the Portuguese priest Pedro Paez in 1618, a fact which the late eighteenth-century Scots explorer James Bruce overlooked when he claimed the honor. But these discoveries had been made before the main interest of the European learned and popular worlds was focused on Africa. The problems did not arouse acute interest until two German missionaries in the employ of the British Church Missionary Society in East Africa made some startling discoveries. Johann Rebmann and Johann Krapf saw in 1849 the snowcapped mountains of Kenya and of Kilimanjaro (Africa's highest, with an elevation of 19,340 feet). Then in the early 1850s a third German member of the society, Jacob

Erhardt, collected information from his companions and from African and Arab travelers which he utilized to complete his famous map indicating that there was a great lake astride the equator—in reality integrating confused reports of Lakes Victoria, Tanganyika, and Malawi.

Stimulated by this flow of information from East Africa the Royal Geographical Society commissioned two British Indian army officers, Richard F. Burton and John Hanning Speke, to proceed to the distant interior upon an expedition to investigate the problems of the Nile sources. The two highly individualistic men followed the usual African-Arab trading route across central Tanzania—they were the first Europeans to do so—to reach Lake Tanganyika in 1858. Since both were ill when they arrived at the lake they were unable to accomplish any significant explorations in this locality. However on their return trip to the East African coast, while Burton lingered among the Arab colony in the important Nyamwezi trading state of Unyanyembe (around present-day Tabora), Speke followed another African-Arab route northward to discover Lake Victoria. Despite the lack of any tangible proof, Speke declared that he had at last discovered the true source of the Nile. Burton's disagreement with Speke's hypothesis was one of several matters leading to a serious quarrel between the two men. Subsequently Speke was given the direction of a new Royal Geographical Society expedition to investigate his theory. Accompanied by another officer, John A. Grant, he visited the important African state of Buganda. His account of this highly centralized polity and its dynamic and cruel ruler, Mutesa I, aroused much interest in Europe. Speke found the outlet of the Nile from Lake Victoria, and then he and Grant in part followed the course of the river on its flow to the Mediterranean. While marching northward Speke and Grant met another exploring Briton, Samuel Baker, who, following information received from the two Nile discoverers, went on to visit and name Lake Albert in 1864, thus partially filling in another important link in the Nile chain. Since, however, Speke had not traveled alongside the entire course of the Nile, he found on his return to Britain that his theory of the origins of the Nile was still subject to valid questioning. More exploration remained to be undertaken, but Speke's untimely death in 1864 in a hunting accident removed him from the resolution of the problem.

The quest continued when the man whom many consider the greatest of all nineteenth-century European personalities active in Africa undertook the investigation of the remaining problems of the Nile sources. David Livingstone left the southern Tanzanian coast in 1866 on what became possibly the most well known of African exploring ventures. Livingstone by this period was near the peak of his African career. Born of poor parents in Scotland in 1813 he had won his way to an education and arrived in southern Africa in 1841 as a medical missionary in the service of the British London Missionary Society. Livingstone discovered that the vital but often humdrum tasks of a missionary resident in one locality were not for him; instead he set forth upon a series of missionary explorations designed to open the interior to Christianity. These travels culminated in Livingstone's great journey during the years 1854-56, from the southern interior to the coast of Angola, and then eastward across the continent to the Indian Ocean coast of Moçambique. The Scots missionary's straightforward recounting of this adventurous venture, undertaken with a few African companions, and without significant financial or other resources, in his

Missionary Travels and Researches in South Africa became an immediate best-selling volume, cementing Livingstone's reputation as the European explorer of Africa with the widest popular appeal. After a series of explorations from 1859 to 1863 along the Zambezi and Ruvuma Rivers and Lake Malawi (which he discovered), in which Livingstone's desire to open the interior to Christian settlement was not realized, he was selected by the Royal Geographical Society and the British government to investigate the remaining details of the watershed of Central Africa.

As he pushed westward from Lake Malawi, instead of reaching the sources of the Nile, Livingstone came upon the ultimate reaches of another great African river system, the Congo. He mistakenly, even perversely since he was so committed to resolving the problem of the Nile, refused to recognize his discovery. As the missionary-explorer doggedly continued his lonely travels various rumors reached Europe concerning his progress. At one instant, it was feared that Livingstone had been killed by raiding Africans. All this uncertainty further raised public interest concerning Livingstone's doings. To profit from the attention which Africa had gained in the public mind the volatile American owner of the *New York Herald*, James Gordon Bennett, commissioned one of his leading reporters to meet with Livingstone in Africa, thus inadvertently paving the way for one of the century's most famous events of African exploration. The reporter, Henry Morton Stanley, a brash, self-made man who had risen from a very humble position in British society, had already won an African reputation for his successful scooping of the reportorial field with his exclusive account of the victorious British expedition of 1868 against King Tewodoros of Ethiopia.

With his usual blend of resolute determination and singleminded ruthlessness, Stanley set forth from Zanzibar to seek Livingstone at Ujiji, a Lake Tanganyika port town which the missionary was scheduled to visit at some point during his travels. By a happy coincidence Stanley reached Ujiji in November 1871 to find Livingstone there and to utter his famous phrase—which he ever afterwards regretted—"Dr. Livingstone, I presume?" More significantly Stanley had arrived to succor Livingstone with companionship and supplies when the missionary was hampered by ill-health and suffering from the loss of expected provisions through the acts of untrustworthy subordinates. By the time that the two men parted, Livingstone, who despite his weakened physical condition had refused to leave Africa until his explorations were finished, was well provided with supplies for his continued quest. And, importantly, Livingstone had made a major impression upon Stanley, preparing the way for the American reporter's future career in Africa.

Livingstone marched on with his African companions in search of the Nile sources, although at times even he began to doubt his goal, until his health finally gave way. In 1873 Livingstone died on the Zambian shore of Lake Bangweulu, a part of the Congo River system. His African followers carried his remains to Zanzibar from whence they were brought to London for a memorable burial, before all the great of the day, in Westminster Abbey. The impact of this dramatic ending of Livingstone's career was overwhelming. It was clear that the missionary-explorer's work had to be completed. And not surprisingly Stanley was selected for the task by the editors of the British *Daily Telegraph* and the *New York Herald*.

In 1874 Stanley once more left Zanzibar on one of the most eventful expeditions in the annals of African exploration. Rushing to Lake Victoria, where, like Speke before him he was much impressed by the Buganda of Mutesa I, Stanley circumnavigated the lake, thus contributing to the solution of the problem of the Nile source. Next proceeding to Lake Tanganyika, where he similarly visited the areas previously left unobserved by European explorers, Stanley discovered the lake's outlet, the Lukuga River, which flowed westward toward the Congo. Then he marched to that great river. Although Verney Lovett Cameron, a young British naval officer, recently had preceded Stanley on this path on his journey across Africa in 1873-74, he had been prevented, as Livingstone had been earlier, from following the Congo towards its outlet on the Atlantic by the Arabs of Nyangwe, a major Arab trading center on the river. But Stanley was not to be stopped. Fighting his way through numerous riverine peoples along the Congo, Stanley finally reached the ocean in 1877, proving that above the rapids which blocked access of the Congo from the Atlantic there was a thousand-mile stetch of waterway suitable for navigation. It had been a remarkable feat of exploration and the knowledge gained was of considerable significance for the coming partition of Africa.

The three river quests, for the Niger, Nile, and Congo, are examples, perhaps the most dramatic ones, of the European and American endeavors to learn the secrets of the African interior. The significant activities of many other explorers working to solve similarly important problems of African geography—such as the scholarly Heinrich Barth, who traveled in the western Sudanic region during 1850-55 or the arrogant Baron Carl Claus von der Decken, who journeyed in eastern Africa during the early 1860s—have not been detailed. Nevertheless the strivings of Park, Lander, Livingstone, Stanley, and others mentioned provide a fair illustration of the accomplishments of the major explorers of. Africa in the years before the 1880s. The basic outlines of the interior were then known, especially the routes of the principal river systems. When this information was available to a changed climate of opinion in Europe, Africa was poised to undergo the headlong rush of the Europeans to gain territorial control of the African continent.

Explaining the Scramble

The reasons for the sudden quickening of European political and economic interest in Africa beginning in the 1880s, a process which led to the loss of independence for almost all Africans by 1914, have been a source of continuous argument over the last three-quarters of a century. Through the events discussed in this study we have observed that the European nations, especially Britain and France, gradually had increased their involvement in Africa all during the nineteenth century. Nevertheless the decade of the 1880s did see the pace of territorial acquisition quicken significantly among the traditional European occupiers of African territory as well as through the intervention of new imperial powers, Germany and Italy, and by the individual involvement of Leopold II of Belgium. Even the long dormant imperialism of the Portuguese was shaken to action.

Explanations based upon economic considerations have remained at the forefront, from the earliest days of this century until the present, of the reasons advanced for the new burst of European activity. Although not fully accepted by most scholars of the Western world, the economic factor is an interpretation favorably received by many Africans. The first important variation of this thesis was formulated in 1902 by a British thinker who had been personally influenced by the course of the Boer War in South Africa (1899-1902). John A. Hobson postulated that, because most of the profitable outlets for capital were no longer open within Europe, financiers had turned to Africa for investments to insure their necessary profits. Hobson affirmed that the working class supported this stimulation to empire, but only because they had been misled into thinking that overseas expansion was vital to their continuing employment. The British writer, however, was not an economic determinist. Economic factors might be to Hobson the "taproot of imperialism," but nevertheless he considered that the policy decisions already made were reversible, and that the financial resources he held were wasted in overseas ventures could be diverted to better the living conditions for the workers within their own countries.

This hypothesis, which included some reasonable arguments, at least as far as the Boer War was concerned, probably would have passed into obscurity—as did the arguments of so many writers on the causes of imperialism—but for its later partial incorporation into the writings of a then unimportant Russian revolutionary exile. Vladimir I. Lenin in 1917 while residing in Switzerland published a brief tract entitled *Imperialism: The Highest Stage of Capitalism,* in which he advanced an explanation for Europe's imperial expansion in terms of economic determinism. The future Russian leader constructed his ideas on those of Hobson and his successors (Karl Marx had given virtually no attention to imperialism). Lenin, in his argument, maintained that by about 1870 opportunities for capital investment within Europe had become exhausted. He further affirmed that bankers had gained control over the capital accumulated by the earlier industrial developers. Lenin's conclusions were that the financiers had turned to the colonial world for outlets for this "moribund capital." He held that the controllers of capital were able to influence their governments to do their bidding in securing safe, restricted colonial markets for their profitable investment. The capstone of Lenin's entire argument was that once the potential colonial territories were finally divided between the great capitalist nations investment capital would once more lack profitable locations for expansion. The result would be a great war inevitably ending in the final downfall of the entire capitalist system and the triumph of the world proletariat through communism. There is no need to belabor the obvious flaws in Lenin's argument.[1] It was proved long ago that most European capitalists were never interested in investing in Africa. And obviously the final result which might have made the argument viable never occurred. No major war ever grew out of European colonial rivalry in Africa or Asia, and the capitalist system, regrettably in the eyes of many, still shows no signs of fading away. If the Lenin of this theoretical study had not gone on to direct one of the world's most momentous social revolutions, the entire argument would have been forgotten long ago.

But if economic hypotheses do not provide the key to explaining the origins of the scramble, what suggestions offer a better explanation? Among the many varied arguments

1. See, for example, Raymond Aron, "The Leninist Myth of Imperialism," *Tha Partisan Review* 18 (1951): 646-62.

elaborated since the partition began, perhaps the soundest one advanced by recent Western scholars develops its thesis along the lines of strategic considerations, with heavy deferences paid to the shifting balance of power in late nineteenth-century Europe. According to this formulation Africa before the 1880s had been largely left free of the seizure of its territory by the Great Powers, especially by Britain, the preeminent world power, because the British policies designed to support free trade had allowed that nation to draw what it wanted from Africa without the unnecessary expense of direct colonial administration. The great early exception to the policy of indirect control—as practiced in Zanzibar, for example—was the British annexation of South Africa in 1815. This step, however, was taken for overriding strategic reasons: South Africa, because of its location upon the route to British India was simply of too vital an imperial importance to let it fall into possibly hostile hands. This presentation, of course, does not adequately explain the heavy French involvement in Algeria, which had no significant strategic importance to France, but then neither do the arguments based upon economic factors, since the North African territory long remained a drain upon the French budget. Algeria was taken simply for the none-too-rational reasons of national and dynastic prestige.

Some scholars have developed a further refinement of the arguments based upon the factors of the European balance of power to answer the difficult questions as to what nation, or individual, initiated the specific events which led to the scramble. One interpretation assigns primary position to Britain's 1882 decision to occupy Egypt following the military intervention designed to safeguard the Suez Canal and other British financial investments. Consequently, the argument runs, the disappointed French government, which for domestic reasons had chosen not to join Britain in the intervention, began expanding its influence in other parts of Africa out of frustration at the continuing British occupation. But this argument does not really recognize the deep rivalry that was already underway in Africa between France and Britain and that the events in Egypt therefore were probably only another episode in an ongoing process.

A sounder hypothesis for explaining the events inaugurating the scramble of the 1880s is an analysis based upon the activities of a new entry into the quest for African territory, Leopold II, the King of Belgium. Ruling his country since 1865, Leopold was an exceedingly talented, ambitious, and unscrupulous individual, a man who found his position as the constitutional monarch of a small, inward-looking European nation too limited for the exercise of his abundant energies and ambitions. Leopold early had turned his thoughts to schemes for colonization with fruitless plans for action in many parts of the world. His final approach, one which had no specific territory in view, but which was designed to provide an opportunity for maneuver in Africa, was the summoning of an international conference at Bruxelles in 1876 to discuss the solutions to the remaining geographical and humanitarian problems in that continent. As the sole head of state present among the delegates from many participating nations, Leopold naturally was chosen the first director of the organization created at the conference, the International African Association, a position he afterwards maintained. The association's aims were stated to be the further exploration and advancement of humanitarian concerns in Africa. Initial ventures were designated primarily for East Africa since there were no conflicting claims of

European nations for territories in that region. From 1877 on a series of largely Belgian manned expeditions, serving the association and not the Belgian government, created stations along the trade route to Lake Tanganyika and on the lake's shores, as part of an overall scheme to reach the Arab-dominated regions of the Congo.

While these activities were progressing slowly Leopold quickly changed his course to take advantage of a significant new happening, the discovery by Stanley of the course of the Congo River. The event, in 1877, opened an opportunity for Leopold to work toward his goal along the length of this great waterway in regions as yet unaffected by any rival European claimant. Thus when Stanley was unable to interest either British public or private sources in his development schemes for the Congo, he entered the employ of Leopold with the initial task of staking out claims for a new organization, the International Association of the Congo, a group completely dominated by the astute Belgian ruler. But Leopold and Stanley were not left without competition in their Congo venture. One consequence of the 1876 confernce at Bruxelles had been the establishment of separate national branches of the International African Association, a step supported by Leopold since it maintained the veneer of his supporting unselfishly plans for African development. Leopold, however, became partially entangled in the web of the "international" effort he had created.

The French branch of the International African Association helped to support a young Italian-born naval officer, Pierre Savorgnan de Brazza, in explorations in the hinterland of the French territory of Gabon along the Ogowe River. The venturesome de Brazza, who had originally conducted explorations in this region during 1875-78, eventually penetrated to the Congo River above the point where Stanley was then concluding agreements with Africans on behalf of Leopold's organization. On his own authority de Brazza in 1880 concluded a treaty in the name of France with an African leader in the vincinity of present-day Brazzaville. When the French traveler returned to the Atlantic coast by proceeding down the Congo he met Stanley; nothing was said, however, of his anticipating Stanley's work. In France the treaty was presented to the government and because of a new, rising interest in African expansion it was ratified in November 1882. The decision meant that a dangerous rivalry had been opened between a major European power and Leopold, the leader of a private organization with only a most tenuous standing in international law.

Moreover this unwonted activity along the river had stimulated into action other European nations with various interests in the Congo region. The Portuguese, basing their claims in part upon the actions of their ancestors within the Kongo Kingdom, had long asserted their jurisdiction over the regions around the mouth of the Congo as well as inland territories. At the same time Britain became interested since its traders dominated the commercial activities of the Congo, centering at the port of Boma; the British trade reached an estimated annual total of £2,000,000 by 1884. The consequence was a treaty of 1884 between Britain and Portugal which confirmed Portuguese authority in the disputed region—between 8 degrees and 5 degrees 12 minutes south latitude—while granting the British the freedom of trade in Portuguese territory. Because of the relative strength of the two powers involved, the arrangement would have insured the existing British commercial predominance. The proposed treaty, however, encountered major opposition—discreetly stimulated by Leopold—from humanitarian factions within Britain who did not trust the Portuguese because of their notoriously lax attitude towards the continuation of slavery and the slave trade. Because of this hostility and because of foreign—especially German—opposition, the treaty was dropped by the British and Portuguese governments. The Congo problem had evolved into a potentially major source of diplomatic friction among the several nations concerned, for various reasons, with the region. Leopold, with no backing other than that of his own organization, had little apparent hope for gain in such rivalry.

Into this growing dispute over the disposition of African territory came a new major European state. Germany, unified since 1871 under the astute leadership of Otto von Bismarck, had not at first manifested any significant interest in colonial undertakings. Individual Germans—many of whom had played an important role in Africa as explorers, traders, and missionaries—nonetheless wished, for reasons suitable to their several callings, or for those of national prestige, to involve their fatherland in Africa. Formal acceptance of a new policy came in April 1884 when Bismarck accepted treaties concluded by a private individual, Adolf Lüderitz, in what became the German colony of South West Africa, a region until then claimed by the British as part of their South African sphere. The reasons for this change in policy regarding colonies are still under debate, with hypotheses being advanced which include Bismarck's internal policies (the chance to gain legislative support from groups striving for colonies) or the machinations of his foreign policy (the opportunity to embroil Britain and France in colonial difficulties so that France would turn to

Germany for support and thus push into the background any policies designed to secure the return of the lost provinces of Alsace and Lorraine). During 1884, for whatever reason, Bismarck continued Germany's colonial advance by dispatching an agent who successfully anticipated the British by concluding treaties which led to the creation of the German West African colonies of Togo and Kamerun. And entering the unresolved Congo controversy, as well as that of the Niger River where there had been acute British-French rivalry, Bismarck suggested that an international conference be called to resolve the outstanding African issues among the European powers. The implicit reasoning appeared to be that Germany planned to uphold the French position.

During the course of the resulting Berlin Conference, (November 1884-February 1885), however, Britain and France did not behave as unreasonable rivals. Questions concerning the Niger quickly were resolved, since before the diplomats met the British National African Company of George Goldie had bought out his competing French rivals. As for the Congo it had clearly become the interest of each Great Power to block others from staking extensive claims to that region, claims which endangered their own rights to unrestricted commerce, and which even more importantly might lead to a major diplomatic confrontation which all wished to avoid. The issue was resolved in negotiations carried on apart from the official deliberations of the conference as one nation after another reached bilateral arrangements with Leopold's organization, thus awarding it recognition as a sovereign political entity. The United States in April 1884, even before the conference began, was the first country to announce this decision. The most important of all the negotiations were those with Leopold's principal rival,

France, through which by February 1885 recognition was secured in return for the right of French preemption of the territory if for any reason Leopold had to surrender his sovereignty. Obviously the French, as many others, were not overly optimistic about the continued existence of the new Congo Independent State. As for the results of the Berlin Conference regarding the Congo, the diplomats created an extensive free trade zone covering much of Central Africa where nondiscriminatory taxes were to be used only for the purpose of meeting the costs of administration. In addition, the navigation of the Congo River was ruled open to all. On the Niger question Britain and France promised to allow free navigation on the sections of the river subject to their respective controls. One other item of note in the final Berlin Act included a statement requiring "effective occupation" for nations claiming African territory, but although this clause has received much notice it meant little since it merely referred to coastal territories and was vague in its wording.

Thus, as was so often the case during the late nineteenth-century Great Power negotiations concerning Africa, quarrels over African interests which had loomed serious, and which could be exacerbated by individuals in Africa, were settled readily enough when the representatives of the European nations involved met in conference. As usual, Africa was not worth a major diplomatic crisis. If Germany did have any schemes to drive apart, for its own advantage, the British and French over African questions, it had failed.

The Partition of Africa

Before and after the Berlin Conference the partition of

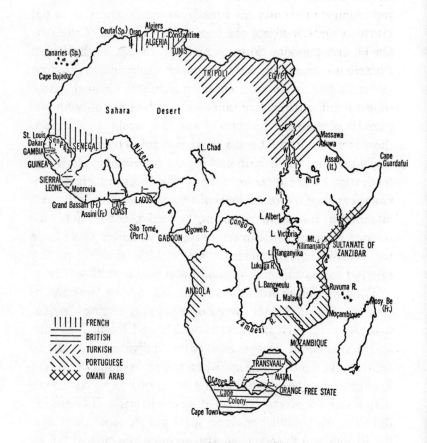

European Territorial Claims in Africa—1880

Africa went forward without causing major friction, except for a few important exceptions like the Fashoda incident, although there were many minor crises begun by headstrong colonial enthusiasts which had to be defused by metropolitan officials. For example, the French, after 1878 left a free hand in North Africa by the British and Germans, but despite an unsettled rivalry with Italy, intervened in Tunisia under the government of Jules Ferry. A pretext was discovered in the "necessity" of containing raiding tribesmen who hit Algerian territory. The intervention shook the unstable Tunisian government, legally a part of the Ottoman Turkish Empire but in practice independent, which had been under the financial direction of a British (Maltese)-French-Italian commission since 1869 because of past financial excesses resulting from the government's mismanaged efforts to effectively modernize its regime. The result of the French move was the Treaty of Kassar Said (Bardo) of 1881 providing for a French military occupation of Tunisia, as well as the control of its foreign relations and some of its internal policies. Further difficulties followed as the Tunisian population resisted the French presence, but the territory was under firm French control by the beginning of 1882. The 1881 treaty, however, was not a sound base for the increasing intervention of the French into Tunisian affairs, especially because of the position of the international finance commission which controlled the North African country's revenues. Through the diligent work of the first French administrator Paul Cambon, a virtual full French protectorate emerged in Tunisia, a situation formalized by the Treaty of La Marsa of 1883.

In East Africa, the establishing of European claims also proceeded relatively smoothly. The British, long predominant in the region, accepted a German intrusion without undue resistance despite the fervid protests of such important men on the spot as their consul general in Zanzibar, John Kirk, one of the most influential of all British agents operating in Africa. Apart from commercial men represented in Zanzibar's busy market from the 1840s who were without imperial ambitions, the German presence dated from spurious treaties concluded in late 1884 in an area behind the north Tanzanian coast by an enthusiastically unscrupulous colonial adventurer, Carl Peters. The Berlin Conference was still in session when Peters brought his agreements, covering lands usually held to be under the influence of the Arab ruler of Zanzibar, to Bismarck. The German chancellor, to avoid upsetting its deliberations, withheld the public acceptance of Peters' claims until March 1885. Caught without preparation, the British, then under William Gladstone, decided that the best policy was to accept the German coup against their Zanzibar ally and even to welcome—at least officially—the newcomers to East Africa. After that basic decision Anglo-German treaties of 1886 and 1890 settled outstanding boundary problems without major friction. And as the British colonial enthusiasts had complained vociferously at their government's initial decision to sacrifice their established position, so did the similar German groups protest when a turn in German policy, following Bismarck's fall from office, led their government to conclude the 1890 treaty with terms, such as the surrender of Zanzibar to Britain, which were held ruinous to the German East African colonial future. In each case the European government ignored the pressure of the colonial interests.

In West Africa Britain and France were the chief rivals; with their colonial territories interspersed throughout the region there was frequent cause for friction. However no major quarrels resulted, although there was for some time an active race for dominion in the Nigerian hinterland. The French from the mid-1880s, after Goldie's National African Company had gained domination of the commerce of the river, had demonstrated little activity in the lower Niger region. But during the 1880s and particularly after their conquest in 1892 of the kingdom of Dahomey, the French became more concerned with inland expansion. An 1890 British-French treaty had drawn a line delimiting their mutual territories from Say on the Niger to Barruoua on Lake Chad, but this agreement did not settle the growing rivalry. Meanwhile in 1886 the British government, in a decision designed to combat French and German rivalry in this region, had awarded a charter to Goldie's company, henceforth known as the Royal Niger Company. When in 1894 the French rushed an expedition to gain possession of Borgu, thus insuring themselves a valuable position on the Niger River, the Royal Niger Company utilized Frederick D. Lugard, well known then for his martial exploits in Malawi and Buganda, to check the French design. The populous territory of the Yoruba peoples, of much importance to the British since it stretched inland behind Lagos, similarly was gained by the British through conquest and diplomacy in the period from 1888 to 1895. When the Royal Niger Company met resistance from the Muslim Africans of Northern Nigeria in 1897, it also had to fear possible involvement with nearby French forces; thus the British government, through the decision of its active Colonial Secretary Joseph Chamberlain, intervened to support a newly created West African Frontier Force. Lugard was made its commander. But although local rivalry between the French and British remained acute, the sounder heads of London and Paris as usual prevailed. The Niger Convention of 1898 ended the extended friction by fixing Nigeria's northern and western boundaries in a manner which largely supported British interests.

Along the Gold Coast the British expanded their control from the coastal trading centers which they had held for centuries. In 1821 their government had abolished the Company of Merchants Trading to Africa, replacing its limited administration by crown rule under the governor of Sierra Leone. But hostilities with the Ashanti of the interior, who had broken the power of the coastal Fanti during the early years of the nineteenth century, led to a British defeat in 1824 which cost the life of Governor Charles Macarthy. Although the British reacted by defeating the Ashanti in 1826, the outcome of the warfare remained inconclusive. In 1828 the Gold Coast settlements were returned to the direction of a private organization, the Committee of Merchants, which expanded its administration during the effective years of rule of one talented official, George Maclean. Lacking any significant military force, Maclean, through agreements reached with Africans who trusted him, secured peace and security throughout the coastal region. As a result the trade of the area tripled during the ten years of his activities. Maclean's arrangements had no legal standing, but an official investigation of 1843 upheld his work. When the British government retook control of the forts in that same year it was decided to continue the existing system, and in the Bond of 1844 the coastal Africans agreed to the continued recognition of some of the principles of British jurisprudence. The Africans, however, did not surrender any of their political authority.

In the succeeding years the British government became increasingly disenchanted with its colonial possessions in West

Africa. A parliamentary commission reported in 1865 that there should be no further extension of British administration in this region, and that, except in Sierra Leone, the British should prepare plans for eventually evacuating their holdings. The latter recommendation was not followed, however, and in the following years the British became more involved in the affairs of the Fanti and Ashanti. In 1872 the British even expanded their holdings by assuming control of the Dutch forts along the Gold Coast. The decisions leading to the transfer had been taken without effective African participation. Along with the Fanti fears of the Ashanti—there had been another Ashanti invasion in 1863—and the parliamentary report of 1865, the change led the Fanti to create a Fanti Confederation at Mankessim in 1871. But the new organization, which had the support of both traditional and Western-educated Fanti leaders, was not to the liking of the local British administration; they intervened to end the confederation's existence. In 1874 the British unilaterally annexed the coastal region, making it a crown colony. The decision resulted in part from a new Ashanti war of 1873-74 in which the Ashanti suffered a major defeat. Additional hostilities with the inland African state occurred in the 1890s and at the beginning of the twentieth century when the British at last annexed the region.

The Portuguese, whose pretensions to dominion stretched across Africa from Angola to Mocambique—one British statesman called them "archaeological claims"—found themselves threatened by other European nations once the scramble began, especially from an expanding British movement from southern Africa. It was a particularly dangerous period for the Portuguese, since as the governor general of Angola in 1877, Alexandre de Almeida e Albuquerque, admitted: "It is sadly necessary to confess that our empire in the interior is imaginary."[2] Nevertheless the Portuguese survived the threats to their position. The British were willing at times to push them to extremes, as they did in 1890 when the Portuguese had to back down in face of an ultimatum over conflicting claims for territory in east central Africa, but on the whole the major powers were content to leave the Portuguese in control of much of the territory they claimed. Thus left free, the Portuguese finally completed the conquest of the hinterlands of their colonies. In Mocambique this was not accomplished until as late as 1918, in Angola not until 1930, and in Guinea not until 1936.

Colonial problems, however, did come near to causing major crises with potentially important repercussions upon the international scene. The episode ending at Fashoda demonstrated the latent dangers which were always present. By the late 1880s the British government had concluded that its occupation of Egypt, which allowed the guarding of the Suez Canal, made it strategically necessary for Britain to control the entire course of the Nile River. There had at first been no rival European threat to the British in the region directly south of Egypt since the people of the Sudan, under the leadership of the Mahdi, Muhammad Ahmad ibn Abd Allah, had driven out their Egyptian rulers after 1881. But from the mid-1890s the French began to plan expeditions to give them a foothold on the Nile. There were many delays, however, before a final French decision was made, and during the interval the British, under the command of Herbert Kitchener, seized the opportunity to begin the conquest of the Mahdist state in the Sudan. While the fighting was

2. Quoted in Douglas L. Wheeler and Rene Pelissier, *Angola* (New York, 1971), p. 59.

underway the French schemes finally came to a head, when Captain Jean-Baptiste Marchand, who had left his French Equatorial base in 1897, arrived at Fashoda, on the Nile, in 1898. But the French officer had only a few followers, and although he bravely refused to surrender to Kitchener, who had arrived at his camp supported with overwhelming force, Marchand's position clearly was untenable. The two European officers, however, carefully avoided any action which might have precipitated a major incident, instead referring the question back to their capitals for settlement. Although there was some talk of war, the diplomats settled the crisis through negotiation. An accord of 1899 recognized the power realities of the Nile region, where Britain dominated the territory by arranging boundaries which denied the French any position upon the strategic river. Once again it had been demonstrated that African questions were not to be allowed to upset the balance of forces in Europe.

Only one African state, Ethiopia, succeeded in halting the European conquerors. Italian colonial enthusiasts had directed their efforts to the barren coasts of the Horn of Africa as early as 1869 when they secured a foothold at Assab. More forward Italian moves did not occur until the general events of the scramble drew Italy into the competition for African territory. Where Italian interests were directed, however, Ethiopia possessed an intelligent and determined ruler, Menilik II, who was very conscious of the dangers to his country from European entanglements. But he did desire European aid to enable his growing state to expand against its African rivals. A principal result of this need for cooperation was the 1888 Treaty of Wichale with Italy. As with many other written agreements between Africans and Europeans, there was discord concerning the exact meaning of important articles of the treaty, with the Italians maintaining, over Ethiopian denials, that they had been given the right to control the African state's foreign relations. In the meantime Italy had strengthened its holdings in this region of Africa, occupying the Red Sea port of Massawa in 1885, declaring Eritrea a colony in 1890, and from the late 1880s incorporating the territory stretching from Cape Guardafui to the Juba River into Italian Somaliland. Continuing friction resulting from the ongoing pressure upon Ethiopia from the Italians led Menilik to denounce the Wichale treaty in 1893. Not surprisingly the Italians then invaded Ethiopia; but they discovered that the Ethiopians were resolute opponents. In 1896 a force of about 20,000 Italians commanded by General Oreste Baratieri faced an army of over 100,000 Ethiopians commanded by Menilik. The Ethiopians, with the advantages of fighting upon their own terrain, were in addition very well equipped with modern weapons. The resulting battle of Aduwa was a stunning Ethiopian victory. The humiliated Italians were compelled to make a peace in 1896 which recognized the independence of Ethiopia, although they did retain their holdings in Eritrea.

The defeat festered in the Italian memory so that the Fascist government of Benito Mussolini in 1935 once more moved to conquer the territory for Italy. With the advantages of modern weapons of warfare—including poison gas and air power—the Italians crushed the Ethiopian resistance of the government of Haile Selassie by 1936. Even though Ethiopia was a member of the League of Nations, where Haile Selassie made a dramatic appeal about the consequences of allowing small nations to be conquered unjustly, the chief Great Powers concerned, Britain and France, already affected by the malaise which culminated in World War II, let Ethiopia fall to Italian ambitions. The new rulers held Ethiopia, which was joined to Eritrea and Somaliland to be called Italian East Africa, until a British-led invasion during World War II liberated the country in 1941.

Apart from the anachronistic Italian victory of the 1930s the partition came to a close in the years just prior to World War I with the European seizure of the two remaining unoccupied territories of North Africa, the independent state of Morocco and the Turkish dependency of Libya. The Alawite dynasty, ruling Morocco since the seventeenth century, had succeeded during the nineteenth century in maintaining their country's independence. But with Morocco's strategic location bordering French Algeria and alongside the narrow entrance into the Mediterranean, the country was a source of prime interest to several European nations, notably to Britain, France, and Spain. The Moroccans suffered military defeats at the hands of the French during their war against the Algerian leader Abd al-Qadir, and from the Spaniards during a war of 1860. Even more dangerous to the Muslim state was the growing European presence within Morocco where, especially after 1860, a resident European community, buttressed by important extraterritorial rights, secured an expanding control over the Moroccan economy. The increasing pressure and the Moroccan efforts to counter it, led to a growing financial burden upon the state, especially during the reign of the inefficient Mawlay Abd al-Aziz (1894-1908). The Moroccan ruler also increasingly lost control of the restless anti-European elements within his kingdom. The weaknesses led to increasing European interventions, a situation rendered all the more dangerous since Morocco became caught up in the balance-of-power diplomacy affecting early twentieth-century Europe. After

1904, when an Anglo-French entente balanced French approval for the British position in Egypt against the British recognition of French predominance in Morocco—Spain was also awarded a role—the North African state's future was sealed. In the face of increasing internal disorder within Morocco the French in 1912 imposed a protectorate upon the sultan, and Morocco, divided into French and Spanish zones, passed under European rule.

Libya, which had been subject to direct Ottoman Turkish rule since 1835, had been looked upon with interest by the Italians since the French occupation of Tunisia. But the varying changes in the attitudes of the major European powers regarding the Ottoman Empire precluded any overt aggression until the twentieth century. Hostilities came in 1911. The Italians were met with determined resistance from the Turks and more importantly, from the indigenous Muslim populations who were effectively led by the locally dominant Sanusi brotherhood. Nonetheless the weak Ottoman government was forced to bow to Italian pressure, relinquishing Libya to the invaders by the Treaty of Lausanne (1912). The treaty did not cause the Libyans to cease their resistance; the conquest of the Libyan interior remained to be accomplished when World War I began.

Along with Ethiopia, although in a very different, less dramatic fashion, one other independent African state survived, and even participated in the scramble for African territory. Black Americans, initially sent and supported by the white-run American Colonization Society, with some support from the administrations of President James Monroe and his successors, had arrived in West Africa in 1822 to found Liberia. The black immigrants were either free persons who had decided that a meaningful life was impossible to achieve in a racist United States or newly freed slaves sent to Africa by their former owners, or by public organizations, since the slave-based society of the South increasingly had no place within it for freed slaves. It is significant that most of the leadership of the American free black community opposed schemes of emigration to Africa, preferring to remain in the United States and working to secure the full rights belonging to American citizens. White reformers, notably William Lloyd Garrison, supported their viewpoint.

Despite many serious hardships, including indigenous African opposition to the American invaders, plus the effects of disease, the various settlements founded at Monrovia, particularly under the effective leadership of Jehudi Ashmun (1822-28), and elsewhere (by societies operating from Philadelphia, New York, Maryland, and Mississippi) were successfully maintained and extended. Liberia received its first black governor, Joseph J. Roberts, in 1841 and in 1847 the unofficial American dependency ended its uncertain legal status, which had led to problems with nearby British Sierra Leone, by declaring its independence. The new polity included all of the American settlements except that of Maryland which did not join Liberia until 1857. The United States government, however, because of the influence of the southern states, did not award it formal diplomatic recognition until 1862. By about this period around 12,000 Afro-Americans had emigrated to the African territory, while approximately 6,000 Africans liberated by the American navy from captured slaving vessels had been added to this total.

The ties of Liberia to the United States, however tenuous, were always of some help in preventing the struggling young state from being dismembered by the European nations interested in West African territory. And the Liberians were not passive observers of European expansion; throughout the nineteenth century they followed a policy of moderate enlargement of their boundaries by extending into nearby African areas where they practiced a system of indirect rule over their African subjects. Since, however, there was no difference of color between the American-Liberian rulers and their African subjects, some assimilation between the two groups always occurred. Liberia, however, did lose over one-third of its claimed hinterland in forced boundary settlements with Britain and France. In the early years of the twentieth century, the result of practically one hundred years' existence for Liberia was a country free from serious international threats and ruled by an elite descended from American-born immigrants. From 1925 Liberia achieved a significant boost in economic prosperity through the heavy investment within its borders by the Firestone Rubber Company. By 1950, when Liberia's economy began to become more diversified, the American company supplied about 90% of Liberia's exports.

Although the African colonies of the European nations were not a cause of World War I, the presence in the continent of the various contending states ensured that conflict's extension to Africa. An early proposal for colonial neutrality was never seriously considered by the belligerents, especially since the German colonies, effectively prevented by British dominance of the seas from receiving any substantial support from the fatherland, appeared to have little chance of successfully resisting invasion. Southwest Africa fell before forces from the Union of South Africa, while Togo and Kamerun were conquered by the British and French troops. Only in German East Africa did an effective German resistance develop. The ingenious German commander, Paul von Lettow-Vorbeck, fought a masterfully directed campaign which fully achieved its strategic goal; the tying down of as heavy an Allied commitment as possible, even though there was little chance of a German victory. Although quickly forced on a defensive, the elusive Lettow-Vorbeck continuously avoided his pursuers in a campaign carried on in German East Africa, Moçambique, and Northern Rhodesia (Zambia); he surrendered his still intact army only after hostilities had ended in Europe. Meanwhile British, Indian, Belgian, South African, and black African troops had all been diverted to the East African campaign. Of course what was good for the German war effort meant disaster for the African inhabitants of the German colony and its neighboring territories. They suffered cruelly from the various campaigns carried on in their home areas and from the onerous occupation of serving as carriers for the several armies where disease claimed a heavy toll.

While the war was being fought, and despite such factors as Woodrow Wilson's Fourteen Points, which had a great impact upon Africans knowledgeable of events in the Western world,[3] agreements were concluded among the Allies to dismember Germany's colonial empire. Along with these decisions went a spirited propaganda campaign, emphasizing the supposed excesses of German colonial rule, which was designed to prove that the enemy, once defeated, was not fit to administer colonial territory. Of course Germany's record in Africa was neither better nor worse than that of any other colonial conqueror. Nevertheless Allied victory sealed the argument. During the peace negotiations, however, Wilsonian ideals triumphed enough to have the

3. See p. 189 n. 4.

outright annexation of the German colonies rejected in place of the creation of a system of mandated territories administered under minimal international supervision through the League of Nations. The lost German dependencies were disposed of in this mannner: both Togo and Kamerun were divided into British and French administered sections; South West Africa fell to the Union of South Africa; and German East Africa, except for the African kingdoms of Rwanda and Burundi which were placed under Belgian mandate, went to Britain. Except for the Fascist aggression in Ethiopia in the 1930s, the partition of Africa was complete.

African Reactions

Africans, with the exception of the victorious Ethiopians and the ignored Liberians, had to decide how to come to terms with the militarily superior Europeans during the years of conquest. Decisions were based upon the particular political organization of the African polity concerned, and upon its position in the existing power realities, as seen by other Africans and Europeans, of its own immediate region. The African responses varied widely, from determined resistance to the invaders, through policies designed to utilize them in local dynastic or multigroup rivalries, to a more or less ready acceptance when their arrival meant salvation from stronger African rivals. In some areas a tangled mixture of all the foregoing alternatives were present.

An example of uncompromising African resistance was the reaction in the 1890s to the British invaders by the Muslim state founded in the Sudan by the Mahdi, Muhammad

Ahmad ibn Abd Allah, and then governed by his Khalifa (successor), Abd Allahi ibn Muhammad. The Mahdi, who had declared his mission in 1881, had rallied the northern Sudanese massed under his inspired direction to expel the corrupt and incapable Egyptian administrators of his region who had ruled since the days of Muhammad Ali. During the 1870s and 1880s the tensions caused by this misrule had been further exacerbated by the policies of the Christian European officials appointed by the Egyptian ruler Ismail. They included the overbearing Samuel Baker, governor of the southern Sudan from 1870 to 1874, and the more tolerant Charles "Chinese" Gordon, who after serving in the south became Governor General of all Sudan from 1877 to 1880. A most important aim of their administration had been to work against the slave trade carried on by the Muslims of the north in the southern Sudan.

The Mahdi's followers, fired by religious and nationalistic zeal, defeated the insufficient and inefficient Egyptian occupiers whose home government was unable to give additional aid because of the unsettled political condition of its own territory. The culminating victory was their capture of Khartoum, where Gordon perished, in January 1885. The Mahdi, however, died a few months after the victory, leaving the task of creating a viable political entity in the liberated Sudan to his followers under the leadership of Abd Allahi. The Mahdist forces, who originally had limitless ambitions, had advanced upon Egypt, but they were defeated by British-led troops at the battle of Tushki in 1889. Thereafter the northern frontier was largely left alone. The Mahdists also failed to drive the British from the eastern region of the Sudan where, from 1886, Herbert Kitchener led the British and Egyptian forces. By 1891 the Mahdists were already acting upon the defensive in this area. But in Egypt the British-controlled government was content initially to leave the Sudanese to their own devices. Evelyn Baring (Lord Cromer), the real ruler of Egypt from 1883 to 1907, rather concentrated his considerable administrative abilities upon domestic reform, having little interest in regaining the vast territories of the Sudan which had little of value to offer in the way of profitable resources. As long as Britain's European rivals left the Sudan free of their intrigues, British policy did not change.

Within the Sudan a theocratic Muslim state, with its capital near Khartoum at Omdurman, emerged which made a fair beginning in providing a capable government for its people. But during the late 1880s British strategic perceptions changed. They began to fear the entry of rival nations into this territory through which flowed the Nile River, the basis of Egypt's prospertiy. A series of negotiations conducted with Germany, Italy, Ethiopia, and others insured the Nile valley to Britian; nevertheless the problem of French ambitions remained unsettled. It was finally decided to resolve all uncertainty by an invasion of the Sudan, designed to return the territory to British-Egyptian control. A modern army under Kitchener carried through the campaign with ferocious efficiency, sealing its victories with a massive slaughter of the Muslim Sudanese resisters at Karari in 1898. Abd Allahi, forced into becoming a fugitive, was killed in 1899. The nature of the campaign was illustrated by an action of Kitchener's after the fall of Khartoum: in one of the most outrageous of deeds in all of the conquest of Africa he had the Mahdi's remains exhumed and cast into the Nile.

In the Sudan there had been no chance of accommodation between African and European. The Mahdi's state, founded

by a leader who regarded himself as the earthly representative of his god, was an entity little capable of a dialogue
with an equally bigoted British government. No serious effort
was made upon the British side to understand the Sudanese
or their way of life, with all being dismissed simply under the
rubric of so-called Muslim fanaticism. Therefore in a contest
of military might the better armed British triumphed to
create after their victory an Anglo-Egyptian—though in
reality Egypt had no rule—government which ruled the
Sudan until it regained its independence in 1956.

The complete misunderstanding and lack of dialogue that
occurred in the Sudan, although present in other areas of
Africa, such as in Benin in Nigeria, was not always typical of
the European conquest of Africa. Often both African and
European wished to avoid conflict, sometimes attempting
efforts for discussion and negotiation. But during the 1880s
and later any *pourparlers* were no longer between equals. If
partitions of African territory had been decided upon during
the course of European diplomatic conclaves, the new European "owner " of the land was merely asking the African oc-
cupant to recognize that his sovereignty had been ended
without his consent. Such, for example, was the case with the
martial Hehe state of central Tanzania. The Hehe had been
formed as a people through a successful amalgamation of
small groupings during the middle years of the nineteenth
century by a dynamic leader, Munyigumba. Their conquests
had been checked momentarily at Munyigumba's death, in
1878 or 1879, by a succession dispute, but within a few years
his equally talented son, Mkwawa, had regained control of
the Hehe, once again setting them on the road to expansion.
Unfortunately for Mkwawa and his people, European
deliberations had by 1890 included his area within German

East Africa. The Hehe were located off the principal routes of trade and communication in East Africa and perhaps because of this partial isolation, they were slow to respond to German overtures designed to incorporate them peacefully in the new colony. The Germans, as most colonial governments, preferred to avoid local hostilities; wars, after all, drained limited colonial budgets, while being potentially dangerous because of the always overextended dispersal of European colonial armies. Also, defeats in colonies were very useful fodder for the ever-present opponents of colonial undertakings within and without the metropolitan government.

Nonetheless German aspirations for the peaceful incorporation of the Hehe failed. Mkwawa and his people were at the height of their expansionist period while in addition they possessed little understanding of the potential German strength since they had had practically no contact with the European newcomers to East Africa. Thus in 1891 the Germans sent an expedition against the Hehe to bring them to terms. Perhaps because of a false confidence grounded upon a lack of knowledge of the martial talents of the Hehe, who generally did not use firearms, the Germans were ambushed at Lugalo. They suffered a crushing defeat, losing their commander, Emil von Zelewski, and most of his troops. It was one of the more striking defeats of a European-led force during the partition of Africa. Nevertheless the German reaction to the Hehe victory demonstrated that occasional European defeats in their colonial territories were of little long-run consequence. From their viewpoint the Germans could not allow the loss to go unrevenged, thus standing as a dangerous stimulus to their other restive subjects. In 1894 a German expedition successfully stormed Mkwawa's capital. Hehe power was broken effectively at this battle even though

Mkwawa escaped, managing to avoid apprehension, and keeping a minor resistance underway, until his suicide just before an imminent capture in 1898.

In other instances the negotiations between Africans and Europeans were more meaningful, with the Africans involved attempting to utilize the Europeans for political aims of their own, although they certainly did not really understand what the presence of the newcomers meant to their traditional independence. Among the vigorous Chagga peoples of Mount Kilimanjaro and its environs there were many independent, fiercely competitive states. They included the Chagga of Moshi who had been in commercial contact with the East African coast since the early nineteenth century. Moshi's ruler, Rindi (usually called Mandara by the Europeans), had thus gained some familiarity with outside ways, and had become aware of the tangible advantages to be gained from foreign sources to use against his Chagga rivals. Consequently, during the period of the European race for control of East African territory, Rindi sought to use European rivalry for his own profit. When a British-inspired delegation from the Sultan of Zanzibar arrived at Moshi to conclude a treaty with Rindi, he accepted the proposal. When a German representative arrived soon afterward, Rindi also accepted his treaty. To the canny African leader it was far better to accept the documents—and the accompanying gifts—of both emissaries since a refusal to either of the missions might have caused considerable friction and could have led the European negotiators to seek out his formidable Chagga rival, Sina of Kibosho. The British and Germans resolved Rindi's dilemma by their treaty of 1886, awarding the Kilimanjaro region to the Germans. This decision, however, did not hinder Rindi's diplomacy. Through his exclusive contacts with the Germans he was able to portray Sina as a foe of the colonial rulers and to utilize their military might to defeat his rival in Kibosho.

After Rindi's death in 1891, other Chagga leaders entered into the competition to profit from effective use of German strength. By a careful policy of devious intrigue, Marealle of Marangu, a talented rival of Rindi's son Meli, managed to involve the Moshi chief in hostilities with the foreign rulers which led to his defeat in 1892. Marealle continued his intrigues to become recognized as the principal Chagga ruler. But striving to divert European predominance to African ends remained an uncertain policy. Marealle's supposed involvement in one of the ongoing plots led to his fleeing to Kenya in 1904 to escape the German wrath. Marealle returned to his home area in 1905, but he remained in the future only one of many local leaders. Meanwhile, the traditional power rivalry among the Chagga leaders had been equally dangerous for the other participants. It was only through bitter experience that the African chiefs of Kilimanjaro learned, as other Africans did elsewhere, how much the powerful colonial intruders had altered the old balance of power of their continuing struggles.

One of the most successful African manipulations of a European colonial nation happened in the Kingdom of Buganda. Before the days of the scramble, *Kabaka* Mutesa I had welcomed the British and French missionaries, arriving in 1877 and 1879 respectively, who had been drawn to his state by the enthusiastic reporting of Speke and Stanley. Although not overly interested in their approaches to Christianity, the astute monarch was concerned with turning as much of their practical knowledge as possible to the advantage of Buganda. But since the missionaries were required by Mutesa to reside at his court, both groups succeeded in converting to their religions many young Ganda in the ruler's service. Mutesa died in 1884, before the influences of the scramble reached the states located around Lake Victoria, leaving the difficult task of coping with the new influences to his eighteen-year-old son Mwanga. Lacking his father's prestige and ability, Mwanga, in a weak power position at the beginning of his reign because of the usual African succession process, presided uneasily over a society split into factions of those Ganda following traditional ways and of those stimulated by the outside influences brought by the Protestant, Roman Catholic, and Muslim missionaries and traders. By a not very adroit course of policy, including a brief but inconclusive massacre of some thirty of the Christian Ganda in May 1886, Mwanga influenced the Ganda following monotheistic religions to combine to expel him from Buganda in 1888. The victorious factions appointed a new *kabaka* to succeed Mwanga, but their unstable alliance led to further unrest ending in the expulsion of the Christian forces from the country. They rallied to the exiled Mwanga and by 1890 a combined Protestant-Roman Catholic grouping had defeated the Muslims and restored a chastened Mwanga as *kabaka*.

The internal disorder did not end with this Christian success. Bitter rivalries divided the Catholic and Protestant parties, which included some of the most talented young leaders of the Ganda. Meanwhile Germany and Britain, in an agreement of 1890, had resolved the fate of Buganda, including it in the British East African sphere. The responsibility for administering Buganda was given to a newly organized chartered company, the Imperial British East Africa Company, which dispatched Frederick D. Lugard to represent it in the African state. At the time of his arrival in Buganda in December 1890, Lugard found the party of the Protestant leaders losing supporters and upon the defensive. They naturally set to work to gain Lugard to their side, proceeding in a very indirect manner since the British officer was attempting to follow instructions which directed him to remain neutral in the intra-Ganda rivalry. But at the same time Lugard had to work at the none too easy task of upholding British supremacy with a very limited military force. The Protestants, effectively utilizing the British missionaries, as the Catholics similary attempted with the French, made their faction appear as a group congenial to British imperial interests. Thus when war between the two bodies of Ganda erupted in 1892, Lugard was maneuvered into intervening on behalf of the Protestants, insuring their victory by his superior firepower. Mwanga had joined the Catholic side and he once more, for a brief period, was forced to flee his kingdom. In the resultant division of the spoils of victory—the offices and lands of Buganda—the Protestants, led by Apolo Kagwa, received the major share, thus insuring their future dominance within the British-run colony. It had been a most successful campaign for the Protestant Ganda leaders, but the British also had little to complain of since they had secured the cooperation of a powerful indigenous elite which acted with them, to its own profit, in governing Buganda.

This cooperation was extended to the larger colony of Uganda, incorporating Buganda and neighboring African states and peoples, formed after the British government took over direct administration in 1894 from the financially troubled Imperial British East Africa Company. As a result the young Ganda leaders were able to exert their influence beyond the boundaries of their own state. They particularly utilized their British connection to triumph over their long-standing rival to the north, the kingdom of Bunyoro. This state had unfortunate relationships with Europeans ever since they had appeared in Bunyoro in the early 1870s as agents of the imperial drive of Egypt southward from the Sudan. To this unhappy tradition of hostility, which was all that the British knew of Bunyoro, was now added the biased opinions of the Ganda. Therefore the British paid scant heed to any wishes that Bunyoro's ruler, Kabarega, a talented and tenacious military leader, might have had for peace. Even with Ganda support, however, it took until 1899 for the British to defeat and capture Kabarega. The Ganda profited from their participation in the struggle by receiving a large section of the conquered state's territory, the land later known in Ugandan history as the "Lost Counties." This success, along with additional benefits gained by the Ganda in many other regions of Uganda, did not turn out to be wholly beneficial for the future of Buganda within the large British-created state, but the Ganda efforts were valid at a time when their loyalties understandably were turned entirely to their own kingdom.

Other leaders of African polities were not as successful as those of Buganda in their endeavors to profit from working with Europeans. In the eastern regions of the area awarded by the Great Powers to Leopold's Congo Independent State, Arabs and Muslim Africans from the 1860s had created an effective domination among the upper reaches of the Congo River under a system designed to maximize their gathering of ivory and slaves. By the 1880s political leadership among the Arabs was in the hands of several individuals, or groups of individuals, each of whom controlled a certain region of the vast area. The outstanding personage among them was the Afro-Arab Hamid bin Muhammad, better known to his contemporaries as Tippu Tip, the most famous of all Muslim exploiters of east central Africa during the nineteenth century.

While Tippu Tip and other Arabs were extending their territories, the officials of the Congo Independent State, beginning with the pioneer efforts of Stanley, entered the Arab-dominated regions. Relations at first were tense, although peaceful, until in 1886 a brash and arrogant British officer in state employ, Walter Deane, forced a confrontation with the men of Tippu Tip—the Arab leader was then absent in Zanzibar—at Stanley Falls, Leopold's most advanced outpost in the Congo. Deane and his men were driven from their station, leaving Leopold's government, since it lacked both sufficient financial resources and military strength for a major confrontation with the Arabs, no alternative but to abandon the post to its conquerors. Meantime the European dismemberment of the Zanzibari sphere of influence had persuaded the pragmatic Tippu Tip to consider carefully the correct policy to pursue to safeguard the future of his Central African dominions. Unlike some of his African and Arab companions, the Arab leader had no innate hostility to Europeans; in fact he had given important aid in previous years to many of the major explorers of the African interior, including both Livingstone and Stanley. At this time Stanley was preparing to embark on a major African venture to bring aid to Emin Pasha (Eduard Schnitzer), a German scholar and explorer who in the employ of the Egyptian government had been cut off by the Mahdist forces in the Sudan. Stanley therefore offered Tippu Tip a position as the representative of the Congo Independent State based at Stanley Falls and the Arab leader accepted. Under the terms of the agreement, Tippu Tip was to work against the slave trade and to insure the profitable development for the state of the ivory trade.

Tippu Tip, once back at Stanley Falls in 1887, honestly attempted to the best of his considerable ability to pursue this new course of policy. But he required the active support of Leopold's officials, since the important Arabs of the Congo who did not accept his authority were not prepared to live up to the provisions of the agreement concluded between Stanley and Tippu Tip. The support was never forthcoming because the Congo State officers regarded the accord merely as an expedient which would be brushed aside as soon as their military strength was developed enough to enable a conquest of the Arabs. The seemingly inevitable episode forcing hostilities occurred in 1892 when an important African lieutenant of the Arab leader, Ngongo Lutete, crossed into territory considered by the Congo State as beyond the Arab sphere. Ngongo Lutete's party was defeated and the state forces under the capable leadership of Francis Dhanis concluded an accord with the African leader whereby he transferred his allegiance to them. Tippu Tip was then once again absent in Zanzibar, but his son and principal subordinate, Sefu bin Muhammed, resolutely decided that this major defection was a direct challenge by the Europeans to Arab power which could not be allowed. Allied with other Arab leaders who equally were reacting to varying forms of European intrusion into their spheres, Sefu marched upon Dhanis. The Arabs suffered a series of defeats, in one of which Sefu was killed, during a well-managed campaign by Dhanis. Other hostilities against the Arabs were carried on along the shores of Lake Tanganyika by members of an anti-slavery "crusade" begun through the work of the French

Cardinal Lavigerie in 1888, which had been absorbed into Leopold's administration of the Congo. By 1894 the Arab domination of the eastern Congo was ended, with most of the former Arab magnates either dead, refugees, or prisoners of war. The way was open for Leopold to organize without hindrance the entire reaches of his state for his own profit.

One other aspect of the initial European arrival should not be ignored. Some African states welcomed the invaders. The reasons are clear. The Nyamwezi of Urambo, for example, the people of the once mighty central Tanzanian state founded by the great war leader Mirambo—called by Stanley the African Bonaparte—had suffered serious decline after the death of their redoubtable chieftain in 1884. Surrounded by aggressive African rivals Urambo grew increasingly weaker. Mirambo's successor, his brother Mpandashalo, bravely strove to reverse the trend, but he met his death in 1890 while attempting to expel a band of Ngoni raiders. Thus when the first major German column arrived among the Nyamwezi in 1890 the leadership of Urambo welcomed them and readily accepted their protection as the only feasible means of preserving the existence of what little remained of their state. On these grounds it was a rational, and successful, decision, although of course the Nyamwezi then could not realize the adverse long-term results of their decision to accept European rule.

Whatever the sequence of events, almost all of Africa was forced to accept the rule of the European conquerors. The differences in military technology between the two sides made this result virtually certain, as did the divided or comparatively small size of the African states resisting defeat. The Europeans, almost always utilizing African troops trained in European techniques, defeated African peoples one by one, often allying with one state against another. Until this fragmentary political system was ended, there was little hope of most Africans regaining their independence.

4   European Colonial Policies

The major European colonial powers each had a theoretical approach to governing "less-advanced" subject peoples which was formulated usually in extreme length by writers, often ex-colonial officials, residing in the metropolitan homeland. At the same time the officials actually working in the colonies were devising policies stemming from the decisions which they had to make to meet the crises occurring in their particular area of responsibility. The two approaches to colonial policy, theoretical and practical, were not always in agreement. This chapter will examine policies in selected African colonies to illustrate the varying methods of administration practiced by the principal European

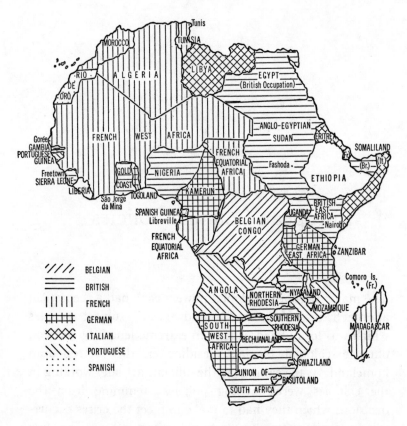

European Territorial Claims in Africa—1914

Legend:

/////	BELGIAN
≡≡≡≡	BRITISH
|||||	FRENCH
‡‡‡‡	GERMAN
XXXX	ITALIAN
\\\\\	PORTUGUESE
:::::	SPANISH

124

occupiers of the continent—France, Britain, Belgium, and Portugal.

French Colonial Policy

In the early twentieth century the possessor of the largest extent of African territory was the government of the Third French Republic. The French African holdings encompassed widely different environments and populations. In North Africa the French ruled Berber- and Arabic-speaking peoples in Algeria, Tunisia, and Morocco. In West Africa the great territory of French West Africa stretched from the Atlantic coastal regions to the desert of the Sahara and the lands around Lake Chad. With its capital at Dakar the federation included eight separate colonies: Senegal, Mauritania, French Sudan, Upper Volta, Niger, Guinée, Ivory Coast, and Dahomey. Further south was another extensive federation, French Equatorial Africa, extending from the Atlantic coast to Lake Chad and the Anglo-Egyptian Sudan. It included the four colonies of Gabon, Middle Congo, Oubangui-Chari, and Chad; its capital was at Brazzaville. The territories along the western coast also included the mandates of Togo and Cameroun. Off the east coast of Africa the French ruled the thousand-mile long island of Madagascar, the neighboring four small islands of the Comoros (Mayotte, Moheli, Anjouan, and Great Comoro), and the equally small island of Réunion. Finally, on the Horn of Africa, the French possessed the colony of French Somaliland. The political and cultural diversity of the African peoples ruled in these many dependencies was immense, ranging from the once highly centralized state of Dahomey to the loose confederations of the Sahara nomads, from the peanut cultivators of the Senegal to the camel pastoralists of Somaliland.

The French first began to formulate a ruling doctrine for their overseas territories during the seventeenth century. It evolved naturally enough from the comfortable French belief in the superiority of their own culture, plus the readiness with which they generally welcomed non-Frenchmen who accepted their culture. Roman Catholic Christianity occupied an important position in this doctrine since the French were seriously concerned with spreading their religion to any new dependencies. French rivalry with the equally concerned Catholic rulers of the Spanish Empire insured an early competition in colonial endeavors.

It was from this line of reasoning that the characteristic French policy of assimilation developed. As applied to some early subject peoples of France, for example the Huron and other American Indians of Canada, it meant that an individual Huron who adopted French culture, including its religion, should receive all the rights of a metropolitan Frenchman. That very few Indians, despite the strenuous efforts of French Catholic missionaries, ever accepted French culture did not vitiate the validity of the principle. Nor did the fact that the French settlers of the sugar-producing colonies of the West Indies—Saint Domingue, Martinique, and Guadaloupe—or of the Indian Ocean Islands of Ile de France (Mauritius) and Bourbon (Réunion), made virtually no organized effort to allow their African slave workers or their descendants to acquire the essentials of French culture. The principle nonetheless survived in such areas as the commercial centers of Senegal. And even in the slave colonies it survived, producing despite all obstacles an individual of the great stature of Toussaint l'Ouverture.

France's first overseas empire, with its important holdings in Canada, India, and the West Indies, mostly had been lost by the close of the enduring hostilities between Britain and France in 1815. But the conquest of Algeria from 1830 revivified imperial dreams; new territories were added slowly to join the few surviving French possessions in Africa, the New World, and the Indian Ocean. It was in the hard-won Muslim lands of Algeria, during the course of the nineteenth century, that France possessed a testing place for the evolution of colonial practices, a situation much complicated by the fact that in Algeria France had its largest concentration of overseas Frenchmen. Because of the presence of this resident European population, when theorists or colonists talked of assimilation there were at least two very distinct meanings involved.

The Europeans of Algeria wanted the assimilation of their colonial homeland into metropolitan France, what is best described as administrative assimilation, so that they could gain the political rights of citizenship and their corollary of local self-government. Thus the European Algerians would escape the restraining hand of the French military, which feared that unrestricted civilian control of Muslim Algerians would lead inevitably to unwarranted indigenous uprisings. The opinions of the military were justifiable since any assimilation policy based upon the reasoning of the settler population meant the application of French legal and other procedures to Muslim subjects who had no understanding of the foreign rules and who, consequently, would have been exploited by the Europeans who did.

Other Frenchmen who talked of assimilation for subject peoples meant in Algeria the adoption by the Muslim, and the few Jewish, Algerians of French ways—the adoption of some local customs by Frenchmen also was mentioned vaguely—to allow the formation of a great Mediterranean French civilization combining the best elements of the included cultures. It was a noble vision, even if it did leave the determination of the local elements to be assimilated to the ruling Frenchmen, but to achieve it dramatic changes would have been required in the character of French rule in Algeria, as well as in the nature of the Frenchmen residing in the colony.

When the Revolution of 1848 ended the regime of Louis Philippe, the new republican government, full of reforming zeal with implications for the French overseas territories, awarded the three coastal provinces of Algeria most of the rights of metropolitan departments, including that of sending representatives to the legislature in Paris. Only French citizens could vote for these parliamentarians. Thus the Muslim Algerians, who were legally subjects of France, had no role within the new system. But this administrative assimilation was merely an assimilation of the most limited form. Europeans resided in Algeria as a dominant political, economic, and social class only because of the presence of the French army. Without continued military support the overwhelming majority of Muslim Algerians would have driven them from North Africa. The administrative assimilation ended in 1852 when Napoleon III established the Second Empire. Except for a brief interval (1858-60) when the colony was included among the charges of a ministry for Algeria and the colonies, Algeria was returned to the effective direction of a governor general subordinate to the ministry of war until the fall of the Second Empire at the hands of the German invaders of 1870-71 brought new changes.

During this period Napoleon III reacted strongly against the ever-present demands of the settlers. By the 1860s the French ruler began to think in terms of what later became in French colonial theory the doctrine of association. During an 1860 visit to Algeria Napoleon was greatly impressed by the colorful Muslim notables turned out by the military authorities to welcome him. He concluded, with a logical reaction, that Algeria was not really so much a part of metropolitan France as its proponents maintained. Instead Napoleon asserted that Algeria was rather an Arab state of which he was the sovereign, as he was of France. The two nations should progress together, he affirmed, but since they were so different, each should develop along its own lines. This sensible interpretation was naturally an anathema to the French Algerians who, despite Napoleon's new approach, never ceased striving for closer ties with France.

Neither did the French emperor's policies counter the inherent assimilationist tendencies of French thought. In 1865 Napoleon issued a regulation which opened the way to French citizenship for a limited number of Muslim Algerians. They had to meet many qualifications, including some which transgressed Muslim law, to gain citizenship, but once this was done the Muslims became free and equal citizens. However, by this period much of the administration of Algeria was carried on by French Algerians, or by Frenchmen with beliefs similar to theirs. Consequently the application of the new law was made as difficult as possible to interested Muslims. It must be stressed, however, that the limited accession to citizenship was not due entirely to the hindrances of French officials. Indigenous Algerians had ample pride in their own way of life which caused them to ignore the opportunity presented by Napoleon. Also, any individual making the change had to encounter a social pressure which characterized those opting for French citizenship as traitors to their own people. For both reasons by the end of Napoleon's reign very little assimilation of individuals had occurred. By 1870 only 194 Muslims and 398 Jewish Algerians had qualified for citizenship.

When the debris of the French defeat by Bismarck's Germany had been cleared, the Third Republic instituted a thoroughgoing change in the policy towards Algeria. From the 1870s into the 1890s, assimilationist policies were given the most extensive application ever advanced by a French government. Algeria was declared part of metropolitan France, with the position of governor general being reduced to that of a figurehead. All of the divisions of the French state—posts, courts, etc.—now included the Algerian counterpart within their ranks. Along with these administrative changes came a new influx of colonists, many of them refugees from the lost provinces of Alsace and Lorraine, to settle on lands recently sequestered from the Algerian Muslims who had risen against French rule in a significant outbreak of 1871.

The change in policy, however, was limited to regulations concerning administrative assimilation. To meet the substantive needs of Muslim Algerians an extensive, and expensive, educational program was required to demonstrate to them the advantages, if any, of somehow joining the entity of European France. The effort was never made. French Algerians remained content to utilize the local revenues they collected, which were largely drawn from Muslim Algerians, for their own objectives. Consequently all during the period of full assimilation the Muslims suffered extensively from the application of European laws of which they had minimal understanding. The exploitation and confusion became increasingly obvious to metropolitan leaders. After the dispatching of a prestigious study commission to evaluate the policies followed since the 1870s, the government ended the assimilation venture in 1896. Some Frenchmen blamed the failure on the supposed inability of the Islamic religion to adapt itself to modern conditions, a viewpoint popular with French settlers in Algeria, but this was not the true explanation for the failure. True assimilation, in the sense of an amalgamation of the two cultures of Algeria, had never been attempted. If the policy had been followed seriously, it might have failed nonetheless since the differences in world viewpoint and lifestyles were so great. This interpretation necessarily remains open. The supposed failure, however, had much influence upon the subsequent course of French colonial policy.

The policies in operation in Algeria, whether for or against the well-being of the indigenous inhabitants, had meantime been influencing colonial developments elsewhere in the French Empire. Since a significant section of the French army always was engaged in maintaining its nation's position in Algeria, many French officers before the expansion of the 1880s formed their initial opinions concerning subject peoples while in that territory. The example of Bugeaud, with his emphasis on adapting policies to the conditions of the local scene, was particularly influential upon future French colonial leaders. One such officer, Louis Faidherbe, who had served in Algeria during the 1840s, became governor of the old colony of Senegal in 1854. As described earlier,

during the long period of French occupation of the West
African territory, interrupted only by British occupations
from 1763 to 1783 and from 1809 to 1817, a significant form
of assimilation had resulted. Nevertheless, at Faidherbe's
arrival Senegal remained a very small and relatively unimportant French dependency with about 12,000 inhabitants—including only 177 Europeans—living principally in the centers of Saint Louis and Gorée. Faidherbe, during
his terms of office from 1854 to 1861 and 1863 to 1865,
revitalized the colony through policies that demonstrated a
rare concern for an accurate knowledge of the local scene. He
looked beyond the restricted confines of Senegal, motivated
by schemes to expand French rule towards the regions of the
upper Niger River. In doing so Faidherbe made contact with
the expanding empire of the great Tokolor Muslim leader,
al-Hajj Umar. There were some unsuccessful efforts at
cooperation between the two growing states, particularly in
regulating the firearms trade, but by 1857 al-Hajj Umar's
drive toward the French dominated area had been checked
by Faidherbe's forces, thus causing the Muslim leader to
turn his focus eastward and therefore leaving the French
holdings secure for the immediate future. Faidherbe also
attempted important reform in the mechanism of French
control within Senegal. To build solidarity of interests with
the indigenous Africans under French rule advances were
made in education, in the application of the law, and in the
creation of an efficient African army. The area holding
French citizenship, however, was not enlarged; in any new
regions brought under French rule the inhabitants became
only French subjects.

After Faidherbe's departure from Senegal the development
of the colony slowed under his successors. The changes

brought by the Third Republic had important effects, however. With the right of electing members to the national legislature restored to Frenchmen in 1871, similar rights were extended to the Senegalese communes of Saint Louis and Dakar-Gorée in 1872. The inhabitants of these areas were once again citizens of France with the right to elect municipal governments, to send a deputy to the metropolitan legislature, and to be represented in the general council dealing with the affairs of the communes. The same rights were given to the inhabitants of the commune of Rufisque in 1880, while Dakar and Gorée became separate communes in 1887. Under Gaston Brière de l'Isle after 1876 the French drive into the interior once more was underway; there were ambitious plans to connect the Senegal and Niger waterways through the building of a railway. Not much progress was accomplished, however, until the years of the scramble when Colonial Louis Archinard carried the French colors deeply into the inland regions.

This limited African experience, added to that gained in their expanding position in Indochina, was the essential core of French colonial knowledge when the great expansion of the 1880s and 1890s began. The policies and principles of assimilation were still talked of, and even followed in a few localities, but the experience of the so-called failure of assimilation in Algeria, joined to a newly developing attitude toward subject peoples, was opening the way for a new theoretical approach to colonial rule. Scholarly and popular interest in non-European populations had progressed steadily throughout the century. The Anthropological Society of Paris had been founded in 1859 and the Geographical (then an all-encompassing term) Society of Paris in 1821, while a whole series of regional geographical societies, at Marseille and elsewhere, were created from the 1880s. The flood of information which was presented at their meetings and through their publications demonstrated the great differences of the human race. Consequently many observers now increasingly believed that any policy of assimilation was an impossible goal. Also present in the intellectual and popular currents of thought of that time was a rigorous racism, increasing in sharpness in the latter part of the century, which placed Europeans, especially northern ones, at the head of an evolutionary scheme of human development. In its extreme form this racist thought made its proponents believe that non-Europeans were so basically inferior that their path to the understanding and adoption of the vital aspects of European culture could take place only in the most distant future, if at all.

Meantime, in the French colonial possessions the officials attempting to govern newly acquired territories were putting the theories into practical form. One of the most influential of the colonial governors was Joseph Gallieni. He had gained African experience in the hinterland of Senegal where from 1877 he had been an active participant in the beginning French expansion into the state of al-Hajj Umar's successor, Ahmad bin Shaykh (Ahmadu Seku). In 1892 Gallieni went to Indochina where his contact with the ancient civilization of Tongking led to an appreciation of the virtues of utilizing an elite drawn from the conquered subjects as a subordinate governing class under French supervison. In this manner the French believed that their limited colonial personnel would be used to the best advantage. And while useful local customs might be maintained, practices held repugnant—in the French view—could be ended, and thus the local population would be guided into whatever reforms were thought necessary for its proper development. This policy of association, however, did not at all mean an automatic continuation in office for all of the traditional officials of the previous independent government; they often were replaced at the discretion of the French rulers by new elites supposedly better trained to govern under French direction.

Gallieni was provided the opportunity to develop such techniques in Africa when he was called upon in 1896 to assume charge of the faltering French occupation of Madagascar. The French long had been interested in this great island—they attempted an abortive first settlement there in the seventeenth century—but they had accomplished little of lasting impact before the nineteenth century. At the beginning of that century one of the island's many peoples, the Merina of the north-central plateau, under the enlightened leadership of the dynamic ruler Radama I, had welcomed European, and especially British, influences in their territory. The result was one of the most effective blendings of African and European ways which occurred in the entire continent during the period before partition. Probably only in Buganda did such a similar thoroughgoing process occur. For example, through the teaching of British and French missionaries, the Merina became literate in a rendition of their own language which utilized Roman characters. They also adopted military reforms, following the counsels of British and French advisers, which made the Merina army the most effective upon the island. Of similar importance was the creation of several manufacturing establishments, based upon European techniques, pioneered by a few French individuals. Most of these adaptations survived a period of intensive reaction to the European presence during the reign of Queen Ranavalona I (1828-61), the successor of Radama I.

The Merina state thereafter maintained close ties with European and American missionaries and traders, all the while expanding the area of its rule until it was possible to claim that it was sovereign of all Madagascar. In fact, however, the Merina never did achieve this total domination.

After the middle of the nineteenth century British influence in Madagascar was predominant for a time: the ruling Merina dynasty even accepted Protestantism as the state religion in 1869. But the French nevertheless maintained their interest, and during the 1880s they actively began to expand their position upon the island. The continuing rivalry between Britain and France was ended by an 1890 agreement through which French predominance in Madagscar was recognized in return for a similar recognition of Britain's position in Zanzibar. After a series of ineffectual military and diplomatic efforts designed to induce the Merina to accept the new status of the island, a major invasion was mounted in 1895 to impose French supremacy. The Merina government quickly capitulated to the invading forces, but the defeat did not signify that the conquest of Madagascar had been completed. When the French attempted to organize their rule in the Merina heartland they encountered further opposition from the Merina, as well as from many of the island's other peoples. It was at this stage of the conquest that Gallieni arrived to direct the French administration.

The new governor, bearing orders from France which ended the Merina's claims to the rule of all Madagascar, decided after his arrival that the Merina dynasty was a hindrance to French policy, especially since he held that it was actively encouraging the resistance to French rule. Acting upon his own authority Gallieni deposed and exiled the ruling queen, Ranavalona III, in 1897. The dynasty ended with her since no successor was appointed. The French government, as so often was the case in early African administration, accepted the unauthorized coup by its governor. Gallieni then went on to impose policies designed to stablize French rule in all of Madagascar. One tactic, known as *la politique des races,* called for the utilization of inhabitants indigenous to the area the French were occupying as intermediaries between the newcomers and the masses of the local population. The Merina, if they had been the rulers of the affected region, consequently were relegated to their own territories. In addition Gallieni followed another tactic known as *la tache d'huile* ("the oil slick"), the occupying of one center in a dispute area and, through peaceful means if possible, developing it in such a way as to induce the inhabitants of the neighboring regions to submit to forces based upon the occupied point.

Backed by the one vitally essential element of any colonial policy, military superiority, Gallieni succeeded through his policies in imposing French hegemony over all of Madagascar by 1905. The French were not seriously threatened again until the major Malagasy rising of 1947. With the initial conquest completed, then began the task of providing an efficient—from the French point of view—administration to govern the island. Many Malagasy were used in surbordinate positions, although local circumstances gradually eroded one of Gallieni's original principles. The earliest inhabitants of the island to acquire a Western education were the Merina, and they maintained their advanced position under French rule. Thus the Merina gradually came to hold a predominant position in the government service.

While Gallieni was developing his policies he had the aid of a young subordinate who had also gained experience in Tongking. Louis Lyautey followed Gallieni to Madagascar in 1897; he was dispatched to bring a southern section of the island under French control. While efficiently performing his duties Lyautey increased his already present predilections concerning the value of a carefully developed policy for the indigenous inhabitants of the colonies. Lyautey had the opportunity to become one of the foremost practitioners of the policy of association when he was selected in 1912 as the governor general of the new French protectorate of Morocco. During his administration of the North African territory, which lasted until 1925, Lyautey stressed a policy designed to maintain and expand, under French direction, the authority of the Moroccan sultan's government. Following the usual practice of association, the Moroccan government was overhauled to eliminate or reform those offices the French considered inefficient. Other reforms were instituted to introduce modern techniques of administration. All of the actions were done in the name of the sultan. Steps also were inaugurated to keep new nonofficial arrivals from too much disruption of traditional Moroccan society: one method was to limit the areas open to their exploitation. The latter policy had a better chance of success than in many other French dependencies since Morocco was not a colony, but a protectorate, and thus legally—at least in theory—Frenchmen had no right to a local voice in the determination of policy.

Lyautey's policies undoubtedly gave the Moroccans a more efficient government, at the major cost of the loss of their independence, but they also revealed the inherent contradictions in the development of a policy of association. If there was such a policy operating in Morocco it was an association between an overpowerful foreign superior who knew best on all important decisions of administration, and a subservient indigenous dynasty and people who had little alternative but to follow the directive imposed upon them. The same fate also had occurred in Madagascar where the local indigenous subordinates to the French, the successors to the deposed Merina dynasty, depended entirely upon French direction. Lyautey himself recogized the problem, asserting of French administrators, including himself: "we have direct administration in our blood."[1] Doubtless Lyautey and his associates were sincere in their tenaciously held belief that association between Frenchmen and Moroccans would lead in the long run to a great improvement in the standard of Moroccan life. But with the then current conceptions of the superiority of the European and his methods over all other peoples, the path to the time when Moroccans could decide issues relating to their own fate was lost in the indefinite future.

The policies of a Lyautey logically might be attempted in a country such as Morocco, where the Europeans had conquered a state whose political forms they recognized as roughly similar to their own, even if they usually really did not understand the local method of governance. But in large parts of France's African empire there were no political entities corresponding with the boundaries given the new colonies. Consequently, when French officials arrived on the scene, they necessarily evolved various solutions to the problem of establishing "effective" government. Holding broad powers of authority, with only limited regulation possible from the distant central authority, the *commandant de cercle* (the French equivalent of the British district commissioner) had much latitude in his structuring of the local political system. If a local dynasty existed, it usually was

1. Quoted in Ralph A. Austen, ed., *Modern Imperialism: Western Overseas Expansion and Its Aftermath, 1776-1965* (Lexington, Mass., 1969), p. 103.

utilized if its members proved amenable to French ways. Nevertheless the place of the African in French employ had changed from that of traditional ruler to that of a salaried official, selected because of his literacy in the French language and his knowledge of modern administration. Thus a consequent decline in their prestige was inevitable. If a traditional ruler were not available, or desirable, the new colonial official followed his own discretion in selecting an African official subordinate to him. In many cases this African did not have origins in the indigenous ruling class. And of course in areas where the form of African government was imperfectly understood—acephalous societies always fitted poorly into European-devised colonial systems—the French simply acted arbitrarily to select a suitable intermediary for dealing with the masses of the population.

In these various approaches to creating a viable local government under French direction the theory of association, or the lingering remnants of assimilation, had little practical meaning. The French, reacting to the logic of the colonial experience, were operating in a fashion similar to the actions of all the colonial powers. Thus most of their African dependents were classed as subjects, liable to the French interpreted rules of African law and ruled by the *indigénat*, a system which allowed, for example, imprisonment for a short time without trial. But, importantly, all during the period of French rule, the principles of the doctrine of assimilation did not disappear. The few schools which were established on the European pattern did train a few young Africans in the then current practices of French education, often operating at this level with an absence of racism which was rare in colonial Africa. Consequently, a limited number of Africans, often the sons of important leaders in the traditional African society, were enabled by their own talents to pass through the onerous examinations which Frenchmen in all sections of the French world had to undergo. If successful, they often pursued their higher education in metropolitan France where, even if they endured scarifying instances of racism, their abilities allowed them to gain the best of what the French educational system offered. Once their degrees were successfully attained it was possible for these French Africans—when such a course was largely unthinkable in the British and other European colonial systems—to exercise a sometimes significant influence within the French colonial, and even metropolitan, administration.

The most effective working of this characteristic tendency of French colonialism allowed the inhabitants of the four communes of the old colony of Senegal to achieve a special rank in the French Colonial system. Even when many Frenchmen resident in Africa had fallen prey to the racist tendencies of the European world of the early twentieth century, the citizens of the four communes, including those lacking any significant French education, were able to exercise an effective participation within the French colonial world. In 1914 the first black African, Blaise Diagne, was elected to represent Senegal in the French Chamber of Deputies. Diagne later also became the mayor of Dakar. Because of the French need for African manpower, this talented African politican, content to work through the opportunies allowed within the French system, became one of France's most important West African colonial officials during World War I. And after the war Diagne developed into one of the leading spokesmen for the French system in Africa, sometimes identifying with it too much to satisfy many Africans. By 1931 Diagne had crowned his career by gaining the position of an undersecretary of state for the colonies; he was the first African to hold ministerial rank.

The crisis of World War I helped to maintain the continuing assimilationist current within French colonial practice. Since African troops had played a significant role on the battlefield during the hostilities, the postwar government decided to "reward" the loyal colonials. A law of 1919 provided new conditions for citizenship for some Africans. Later, in another continuation of assimilationist ideas, a reforming French government attempted to counter the steadfast efforts of French Algerians to exploit their Muslim neighbors. The government of Léon Blum attempted in 1937 to pass a law to allow about 21,000 Muslims to receive citizenship. But by this date the North African colonial interests held an entrenched enough position within the unstable French political structure to defeat the proposal. They regarded the attempted reform, as limited as it was, as dangerous, since even the smallest concessions to the Muslim Algerians were regarded as a threat to the European hold in their territory.

Thus by the outbreak of World War II the French concept of assimilation, however venerated in principle, had succeeded only in producing a very narrow African elite capable of living with and understanding French culture. There were, for example, in 1939 only about 8,000 French citizens of Malagasy origin among the 4,000,000 inhabitants of Madagascar. Nevertheless this approach to colonial rule remained without precedent in foreign-dominated Africa. Buttressed by the characteristic French ideals of individual freedom, the few Africans who had drawn the fullest advantages from the colonial system went on to become the natural leaders of the first significant anticolonial movements occurring within the French Empire during and after World War II.

British Colonial Policy

The British ranked second to the French in the territorial extent of their African empire, possessing regions equally as varied in environment and population. Along the West African coast the British ruled the colonies of Sierra Leone, Gambia, Gold Coast, Nigeria, and the mandates of Togo and the Cameroons. In northeast Africa were Egypt, British Somaliland, and the Anglo-Egyptian Sudan. Along the East African shore were Kenya, Tanganikya, and Zanzibar. To the north of Lake Victoria was Uganda. In south and central Africa were Bechuanaland, Basutoland, Swaziland, Northern and Southern Rhodesia, and Nyasaland, and after 1910, the Union of South Africa as a dominion within the empire. Finally, to the east of Madagascar, was the isolated island of Mauritius.

Environments ranged from the lush vegetation of the coral island of Zanzibar to the bleak desert regions of the northern Sudan, from the dense rain forests of the Cameroons to the elevated dry plateau of Northern Rhodesia. Political organizations varied from the acephalous systems of the Ibo of Nigeria, the Kikuyu of Kenya, and the Lugbara of Uganda, to the highly organized polities of the Emirates of Northern Nigeria, and the kingdoms of Buganda and the Lozi of Northern Rhodesia. Clearly, as was the case in the French African empire, no one theory of imperial rule could possibly encompass the entire African empire of the British.

The principal British formulation of twentieth century colonial rule developed around a practice known as indirect rule, an approach roughly similar to France's association concept since it entailed the governing of African subjects through their own rulers. The two nations shared the absence of any conscious policy of preparing their subjects for an ultimate independence. As Philip Mitchell, governor of Uganda, said in 1939: "We have an almost unlimited time in which to make out dispositions."[2] One special characteristic of British rule, however, was that each colonial governor was granted far more autonomy of action than his counterparts in any other colonial African territory. Even though Theophilus Shepstone, a British administrator in Natal during the 1840s had followed a policy of indirect rule, the important formulation of this practice was given by Frederick D. Lugard as a result of his experiences as the first British conqueror and administrator of the Muslim states of Northern Nigeria. Lugard presented his approach in his influential volume, *The Dual Mandate,* which was published in 1922. The system was a rational one for Lugard to develop in his colonial sphere. The old city-state organization of the Hausa peoples of Northern Nigeria had been encompassed in the successful Muslim conquests in that region stimulated by the preachings and leadership of Uthman dan Fodio in the early years of the nineteenth century. The effective unity of this conquest state—covering about 180,000 square miles it was the largest in nineteenth-century West Africa—which had been founded in a great burst of religious enthusiasm had not long endured. Nevertheless the various components

2. Quoted in R. C. Pratt. "Administration and Politics in Uganda, 1919-1945." in Vincent Harlow et al., *History of East Africa,* Vol. 2 (Oxford, 1965), p. 484.

of the state continued to render at least a nominal homage, including the paying of tribute, to the Muslim ruler of Sokoto. There were clear lines of administrative responsibility within each segment of the loose political system. The rulers of the several states—there were fifteen major emirs—in theory held absolute power. They were advised by councils of their vassals or by appointed officials. Below the council district or village leaders were generally chosen by methods traditional to their areas, although the chosen official had to be accepted by the council. And even if the Muslim empire of Northern Nigeria was in decline by the latter years of the nineteenth century, it was to Europeans an understandable and impressive polity.

With his actions limited by the very few Britons under his command, and by a limited budget, Lugard sensibly decided to work as closely as possible with the Muslim hierarchy of the territories which he had just subdued. It was envisaged that the basic political structure of the emirates would be maintained, except for those changes required for reasons of efficiency and morals—as decided by the British. To Lugard and his subordinates, the Northern Nigerian system provided a very effective base for sound government, and to them it was clearly the best system to follow to provide the stable rule which they planned for the benefit of their African subjects. The Africans were to be directly served by their traditional rulers, who were to interpret the new circumstances of British overrule to them in the terms of their own culture. Nevertheless the inherent contradictions of the system were the same in Northern Nigeria as in Lyautey's pattern of rule for Morocco. The real rulers were the British, and everyone was in no doubt as to their ascendency. If unwise measures, in the opinion of the traditional rulers, were proposed they still had to be carried out if the British insisted upon their validity. And if African rulers proved unamenable to British advice, or did not meet the standards the British required for rulers, they were removed to be replaced by other more tractable members of the traditional governing class. The British did argue that this system was teaching Africans how to modernize their states but, when essential directions stemmed from foreign rulers of a different culture, this goal proved largely impossible of achievement, particularly since the British always demonstrated a great distrust for the few Northern Nigerians educated in western ways. Such Africans, in the words of an African editorial, were regarded in all of British Africa as "an inconvenient class to the powers that be."[3] Consequently they never were given the most responsible positions. Nonetheless the supposed merits of the policy of indirect rule were dear to the British and a conscious effort was made to extend the principle to other parts of their African empire.

The East African mandated territory of Tanganyika was one dependency where indirect rule was attempted as a major technique of imperial rule. The immediate British successors to Tanganyika's German rulers had begun applying practices of indirect rule from the earliest days of the new administration. Then, in 1925, Donald Cameron, who had served in Nigeria, became the governor of Tanganyika; he remained in the colony until 1931. Cameron was one of the most devoted upholders of the principles of indirect rule. But in this war-ravaged colony, as in many of the other British territories in Africa, there were considerable difficulties to

3. Quoted in K. W. J. Post, "British Policy and Representative Government in West Africa, 1920 to 1951," in L. H. Gann and Peter Duignan, eds., *Colonialism in Africa, 1870-1960,* Vol. 2 (Cambridge, 1970), p. 38.

surmount in the applying of the policies originally practiced in Northern Nigeria. Tanganyika's boundaries did not include many large-scale, centralized political entities: a 1927 compilation listed 679 recognized tribal authorities within the territory. The Germans had maintained the centralized organization of such states as Rwanda and Burundi (transferred to Belgium after World War I) and of the Haya, but most other similar polities within Tanganyika had suffered considerable alteration of structure from their administration. A typical case was that of the once-powerful Hehe. After the Germans had driven the Hehe ruler, Mkwawa, from his capital, they attempted to rule his state through the appointment of a new ruler of the royal line. But resistance to the Germans did not cease while Mkwawa continued unapprehended. Thus in 1897 the new ruler was executed by the Germans who then endeavored to rule the Hehe by means of non-Hehe African-appointed officials. This policy was maintained until the British reconstituted the Hehe state as part of their effort to follow the practices of indirect rule.

More difficult to achieve was the application of these practices to the many small societies of Tanganyika which often had no political structure above the heads of clans. Faced with the multitude of varyingly governed polities, the British appointed rulers, often from outside of the traditional political system, while gathering together other groupings into administrative units which they considered of the proper size. The changes might have appeared satisfactory when portrayed upon government charts of organization in the colony's capital, but the newly designated African leaders often were not well thought of by the Africans over which they ruled. The latter continued to render deference to their traditional leaders and to their customary courts, even if both had no recognition within the British system. Continuing reorganizations were attempted by Tanganyika's rulers to increase the functional efficiency of indirect rule, but to the end of the British-imposed style of government major problems remained in the creating of an administrative machine supplying the efficiency which the British wished to create. Cameron, however, who recognized the inherent difficulties affecting African participants in a system of indirect rule, was successful in some of his other policies. Tanganyika's government was a leader among British African administrations for its regulations concerning African workmen. To mitigate the hardships facing the laborers, most of whom had to leave their home areas for employment, careful studies were made resulting in regulations governing medical care and the conditions of travel to and from the work centers.

Another variant of indirect rule was attempted in the East African colony of Uganda where the well-organized state of Buganda provided one of the most interesting reactions of an African people to the British rulers. The original agreements of the early 1890s between the Ganda and the British had left the interior workings of the Buganda administration largely in the hands of its own leadership. Toward the end of the decade, however, the British Foreign Office, which then had the responsibility of administering Buganda, desired to arrange affairs so that the expenses imposed upon the British treasury by the African territory would be reduced. A special mission under the direction of Harry Johnston, one of Britain's most experienced and talented colonial officials, was dispatched to Buganda to negotiate with the African regents who managed affairs in the name of the infant Ganda ruler, Daudi Chwa. In Buganda Johnston encountered an African team of negotiators which was fully capable of holding its own in the discussions with his mission. The Africans met the British virtually as equals. Their long experience of European contact and education, largely the work of missionaries, was obvious. The trying times of the Ganda civil wars, from which the regents and their supporters had emerged victorious, also made them very little disposed to sacrifice their predominant position within their society without an adequate return.

In the end, to secure his goals, Johnston concluded the well-known Buganda Agreement of 1900 with the Ganda leaders. It secured substantial gains for the ruling elite of the African colony. In a state where the ruler once had controlled all of the land, the private holding of landed property was now initiated, with the victorious elite of the 1890s securing the principal share of the change. In other clauses of the accord the Ganda leaders, in return for subordinating their state within the colony of Uganda, were allowed very significant powers of local control. The British, of course, remained the predominant power, with rights of intervention, but with their limited colonial personnel it was not until the 1920s that their attitude toward the agreed-upon system led them to any active measures to counter the extensive self-rule of the Ganda. The 1900 agreement was a rare example of Africans being conversant enough with European policy methods—and goals—to enable them to meet the Europeans in a fair negotiation and to secure a result which satisfied the basic desires of both parties involved. Nevertheless, if the practice of indirect rule involved the utilization of traditional African political systems, this end was not a result of the agreement, despite the allegation sometimes advanced that the early British administration of Buganda was "a classic case of indirect rule."[4] The Buganda of the period before 1890 had been governed by an autocratic *kabaka* who dominated most of the activities of his kingdom. After 1900 the *kabaka*—partly because of his extreme youth—instead held a greatly reduced position, while a new class directed the affairs of Buganda. As in most of British Africa, the realities of the local political system, plus the limited number of British colonial officials—there were only about fifty in Uganda in 1919—were the deciding factors of political evolution rather than the principles of any general theory of rule.

Both the British and the French approaches to the rule of African peoples were complicated by the presence of their nationals, with their persistent claims for special privileges based upon their membership in the ruling nation, as settlers within some of their colonies.[5] The most difficult source of settler problems for the British was the European community of the colony of Kenya. There was also a substantial European population in Southern Rhodesia, but there the British stepped down from their position of responsibility for the African inhabitants by awarding full internal self-government to the European minority in 1923. The decision proved a tragic error which had led to the still-continuing hardships endured by the African mass of Southern Rhodesia's inhabitants.

4. Donald Rothchild and Michael Rogin, "Uganda," in Gwendolen M. Carter, ed., *National Unity and Regionalism in Eight African States* (Ithaca, 1966), p. 342.

5. The troubled and turbulent history of the settler populations in Algeria has already received sufficient attention in this volume as an illustration of the problem which the French had to encounter. Fortunately for the French, and for their African subjects, their other areas of European settlement in Africa were limited, except for Senegal, with a European pop-

The territory of Kenya, which was called British East Africa before 1920, was acquired by the British largely through agreements with Germany of 1886 and 1890 that demarcated basic boundaries. The coastal regions of Kenya were incorporated by the legal fiction of their being leased from the hapless Arab ruler of Zanzibar, who had lost his independence to Britain in 1890. The original task of governing the new dependency was shouldered by the Imperial British East Africa Company (IBEA), a chartered company directed by the Scots philanthropist William Mackinnon. The IBEA, which received its charter in 1888, also had the initial responsibility for administrating Buganda. Although the IBEA was grievously undercapitalized—it began with only £240,000—it nevertheless attempted to insure that Britain was represented in the European colonial expansion into the eastern part of Africa. The company attempted some development schemes along the Kenyan coast, where little that was lasting resulted, but its main resources were applied to activities in the supposedly rich interior kingdom of Buganda. The IBEA efforts there under the command of Lugard, which have been described previously, did secure the country for Britain. At the same time, however, they involved a heavy cost which the company, drawing little profit from East Africa, could ill afford. Finally the continuing adverse financial condition of the IBEA caused it to

ulation of over 30,000, the Ivory Coast with about 20,000, and Madagascar with about 40,000, at the time of their independence in 1960. In most of the colonial territories—of course including the four communes of Senegal with their special political position—the settlers had to be given some role in local affairs. But essentially they were normally only a minor problem which could be handled without exceptional difficulty. Most importantly, the settler position outside of Algeria did not lead to a lasting harmful influence upon the relations between Africans and Europeans.

relinquish its charter, leading the British government, after some initial hesitation, to assume direct control of Uganda in 1894 and British East Africa in 1895.

The first concerns of the imperial administration of Kenya were to maintain the route to Uganda and to begin the profitable economic development of the colony. A major step toward attaining both these goals came with the 1895 decision to build a railroad from Mombasa, Kenya's principal port, to Uganda. This difficult technical task, which in one section of the line required the crossing of the 9,000-foot high Rift Valley, was completed—to Kisumu on Lake Victoria—in 1901. The railroad gave a backbone to Kenya, whose territory was increased in 1902 when the Eastern Province of Uganda, containing a fertile highlands region, was transferred to Kenya to insure that the railroad was completely under one colonial administration. But the railroad's successful completion opened a whole new series of problems for the rulers and inhabitants of the colony. The railroad building had been expensive: the original sum voted for the construction was £3,000,000; the final cost was £7,909,274. Kenya's administrators obviously had the task of creating resources to help support its costly administration. The colonial rulers decided that the products of Kenya's African agriculturalists, many of them not yet firmly under British administration, could not contribute significantly to colonial development, thus reducing the subsidies which Kenya had to receive from a reluctant British treasury. Instead it was thought necessary to find other sources of revenue. Indian immigration had introduced a new and ambitious people into the country, particularly in commercial affairs; some officials suggested increasing the

Indian population still further. In the end, however, a decision was taken to encourage the immigration of Europeans.

A few Britons had early become aware of the possibilities for settlement in the healthy highlands of Kenya; notable among them was the future leader of the settler community, Lord Delamere. He first visited the country in 1898 while on a hunting trip originating from Somaliland, settling permanently in Kenya in 1903. During the governorship of Charles Eliot (1901-04), the basic decision to support increased European settlement was made, a policy related to the governor's clear opinion about the African inhabitants of his colony. Eliot said: "We should face the undoubted issue—viz., that white mates black in a very few moves. . . . There can be no doubt that the Masai and many other tribes must go under. It is a prospect which I view with equanimity and a clear conscience. . . ."[6] Among the measures taken which were indicative of future policies was the sending of a special mission to South Africa in 1903 to encourage individuals dislocated by the Boer War to seek opportunities in Kenya. The South African response was enthusiastic enough to require an unprepared Kenyan government to rush through surveys to make land available for the newcomers. The quick measures, undertaken in the rich Kikuyu lands not far from Nairobi (then seemingly unoccupied because of a recent famine), prepared the way for many problems of the future.

The settler community soon became a fixed feature of Kenyan life. With a size sufficient to make an impact upon local colonial officials—there were about 1,500 Europeans in the colony by 1908—its members began pressing for political

6. Quoted in George Bennett; "Settlers and Politics in Kenya, up to 1945," in Harlow, *History of East Africa,* Vol. 2, p. 271.

advantage. They soon made important gains. In 1906, for example, the so-called Elgin pledge (Lord Elgin was the colonial secretary) was issued following settler demonstrations protesting against the allowing of Indians to hold land in the area of the White Highlands. Although the pledge had no legal standing, it did promise the settlers exclusive rights, and it was a promise that was kept. The settlers also sought representation in the colony's legislative council (founded in 1907) through the direct election of representatives from their ranks. This was a natural course of endeavor, the common step on the path usually followed in Britain's overseas settlement colonies on their progress to internal self-government.

But there was a complicating factor in Kenyan society which hampered the settlers' proposals: they were not the only significant alien grouping resident in the colony. Indian merchants had been active for centuries along the East African coast; a few members of this community even had participated in the interior caravan trade of the nineteenth century. The building of the railroad to Lake Victoria had been made possible by the importation of Indian labor—in 1898 there were 13,000 Indian workers in Kenya. Most of the workers, however, had returned to their homeland when their contracts expired. But the opportunities opened for commerce by the railroad led to a new immigration of Indians into the British colony. Enterprising individuals penetrated to all sections of the country to found a trading network of great value to Kenya's development. A few Indians also had attempted to take up agricultural pursuits, although as early as 1903 Governor Eliot on his own authority had issued orders designed to prevent them from acquiring land. The presence of the Indians was not welcome to the resident Europeans. The delusion of European racial and moral superiority, common to most settler communities of their era, naturally applied to Indians as well as to Africans. It was loudly asserted that the qualities necessary for the "proper" advancement of the Africans of Kenya were found only among Europeans. But perhaps what bothered the British settlers most of all was the ability of the Indians to better them in commercial competition. Often coming from the poorer strata of their subcontinent, the Indians were prepared to work longer hours, to accept a lower profit margin, and to inhabit inferior lodgings than the Europeans. Consequently the Europeans quickly organized to limit or prohibit Indian immigration. In return the Indian leaders, acquainted with British principles of law and government, began an active defense of their position based upon their supposed rights as fellow members of the British Empire.

The East African campaign of World War I, involving most of Kenya's inhabitants no matter what their origins, temporarily mitigated the crisis. The war, however, somewhat strengthened the Indian cause because of the important contribution India made to Britain's war effort. But the Europeans profited more heavily since their leading position within Kenya's economic and political life made their wartime cooperation vital. Largely because of this cooperation the Europeans in 1920 achieved the elected representation in the legislative council which they had long desired. This development in Western-style government had made little impact upon the Africans of Kenya, but the Indians were fully prepared to protest against the increased local role of the settlers. The continuing crisis between the two groups of immigrants led to serious friction within Kenya. At one troubled period the settlers even formulated a plan to kidnap the British governor to demonstrate the seriousness of their opinions. The continuing unrest finally caused the British government to come to a decision. In 1923 the colonial office issued the Devonshire White Paper. In it the settlers' goals of immediate self-rule were rejected, thus saving Kenya's Africans from the fate of the indigenous populations of Southern Rhodesia. The Indians were granted the right to elect representatives to the legislative council. A closing statement of the white paper which drew much attention asserted that the interests of the numerically overwhelming African population of the colony were paramount. This statement, with the absence of any concrete policy regarding its meaning, was of limited value, but nonetheless the momentary checking of the settlers' aspirations was a worthwhile victory for the Africans and Indians of Kenya.

Nevertheless the European community clearly remained dominant within Kenya. The Africans, hampered by the inadequate beginnings of a system of Western education, were not given any role in Kenya's central government. The Indians, since they were relegated to a minority position in the legislative council, had many members of their community refuse participation in political life. There was no essential change in this system, which allowed the politically dominant European settler group to direct the expenditure of the colony's financial resources to their own benefit, until the period after World War II. Even then it required a major uprising of Africans, caused by the almost total frustration resulting from their unsuccessful demands for change, to lead the British government to a decided change in policy.

In ruling the African populations of Kenya the British utilized a policy of direct rule, despite the efforts of Percy Girouard, a follower of the ideas of Lugard, who became governor in 1908 after an African career which included the governorship of Northern Nigeria. Since the African polities included few centralized states, the basic unit of rule being instead the heads of small clans or lineages, or the local councils of age-set societies, the colonial rulers were unable to find the authority figures required by indirect rule. At first, therefore, the colonial administrators selected cooperative Africans to aid their rule, men who often were not from traditional lines of authority. But by the end of the first decade of the twentieth century this approach had not resulted in an efficient system of government. Councils of elders, more in tune with the local political realities, were then utilized, although this solution also did not function satisfactorily since the councils were expected to perform in spheres beyond their traditional competencies. Thereafter even if Africans were used in administration, the British abandoned the idea of indirect rule for a more direct system of African governance. From the mid-1920s local native councils were in operation. Under the direction of a British district commissioner they had an elected majority chosen to represent local interests. Even though the councils offered an outlet for the energies of some of the new African generation, they had little effective power. Nevertheless they did accomplish some useful work in the local matters they were allowed to deal with. Similarly both Southern and Northern Rhodesia (apart from Barotseland) were administered under direct-rule policies—although later largely unsuccessful efforts were made to move to indirect rule in the latter colony.

To the south of Kenya, in Tanganyika, the settler problem took a different turn, in part illustrating the influence that a League of Nations mandate exercised. An important and influential German settler population had been present in the colony before the results of World War I brought a change in administrations. The settlers numbered over 5,000 in 1913, a figure roughly similar to the contemporary European population of Kenya. The German defeat led to the expulsion of their settlers, as well as to the expropriation of their property. And once Tanganyika became a mandated territory under British rule certain regulations affected immigration: all citizens of members of the League, including India, had the right to enter the territory without hindrance. Thus a settler community of a more varied national character than that of Kenya emerged. Also, since under the League's charter there was no question over the paramountcy of African rights, the resident Europeans never were able to gain a dominating position in Tanganyika's political life. Finally, because at various intervals before World War II there was discussion of returning Tanganyika to Germany, many prospective settlers were influenced against risking their fortunes in face of the uncertainties of the future. This is not to say that British inhabitants among the settler community did not exercise an influence out of proportion to their size, particularly in the legislative council where they utilized their position in matters of taxation, but they nevertheless were not numerous enough to offset the nature of the mandated form of government. The workings of this system were principally responsible for allowing the less-developed Tanganyika to become the first British administered East African territory to achieve independence after World War II.

Belgian Colonial Policy

The Belgians developed their colonial policy through circumstances far different from those of the British and French. They originally had only one colony, the Congo, a huge territory of over 900,000 square miles stretching from the Atlantic Ocean to Lake Tanganyika and from Northern Rhodesia and Angola to Oubangui-Chari and the Anglo-Egyptian Sudan. The unfortunate history of this territory while ruled by Leopold's Congo Independent State (1884-1908) certainly had much to do with the later character of Belgian rule. As absolute ruler of the Congo, Leopold by the 1880s had invested most of his personal fortune in endeavoring to develop his African empire. But the initial lack of exportable commodities, apart from ivory, made the anxious monarch seriously in need of additional financial resources. Between 1887 and 1895, the Belgian government did provide important loans to Leopold's African government, but the Congo territory nevertheless remained fiscally unstable.

Meantime Leopold had promulgated secret restrictions giving his officials the duties of insuring that they controlled the available resources of the Congo—notably ivory and wild rubber. Large areas of the territory became the private domain of the state, while other regions were shared by the state with large private commercial enterprises. Eventually wild rubber, in which the Congo had abundant resources, and for which there was then a major world demand, allowed the financial state of the colony to take a prosperous turn. By 1910 the African territory was providing one-tenth of the world's output of rubber. The concomitant increasing control of all trade by Leopold's administration made a mockery of the provisions of the Berlin Act of 1885, but the signatory powers at first took no noteworthy action to protest the change.

Eventually, however, the administration of the rubber trade brought Leopold's whole colonial scheme into disrepute. The small staff of Europeans administering the large territory, most of them with limited previous experience in colonial affairs, became responsible for serious excesses against the African inhabitants of the Congo. Reports made by Protestant missionaries, and especially that by British consul Roger Casement in 1904, plus the efforts of E. D. Morel and the Congo Reform Association, publicized these horrors to an appalled world. Many Belgians, with some justification, considered that the British, the most vocal of the criticizing nations, were motivated by their own selfish interests regarding the Congo. After all, they affirmed the British did not have a blameless record in their own colonies. Nevertheless the international origin of Leopold's mandate to rule through the Congo Independent State compelled him to pay serious heed to the charges. Investigatory commissions proved many of the accusations to be true, particularly those concerning excesses perpetrated by the unsupervised African subordinates of the Europeans in the enforcement of the regulations requiring Africans to harvest rubber for the state. All these events forced the start of a process which ended in Leopold being pressured to terminate his personal rule of the Congo Independent State. The African territory became a Belgian colony in 1908.

After Leopold died in 1909, the new administration of the Congo immediately began correcting the faults of the Leopoldian system. There soon developed what many colonial observers considered to be one of Africa's model colonies. The Belgians followed a very paternalistic pattern of direct rule in the Congo, a system which gave both the European residents—there were 35,000 in the period after World War II—and the Africans little participation in the direction of colonial affairs. Only in the League of Nations mandated territories of Rwanda and Burundi, which possessed centralized African states, did the Belgians practice a system of indirect rule. But in the Congo the Belgians undertook the creation of a thoroughgoing policy, probably the most comprehensive in Africa, designed to lead to the social and economic betterment of their African subjects. Included in the policy were broad opportunities for African education, mostly in missionary-run schools, designed to train the indigenous inhabitants for subordinate positions within the colony. Until the period of decolonization after World War II, the Belgian colonial edifice, buttressed by the wealth received from its copper, gold, and diamond-mining industries, gave an impression of great stability.

Portuguese Colonial Policy

At the beginning of the twentieth century Portugal held the African territories of Angola, Moçambique, and Portuguese Guinea. The old and somnolent empire of the Portuguese had been badly shaken by the events of the scramble. But even though the Great Powers, in Portuguese eyes, had seized unjustly regions rightly theirs, Portugal had been left with a significant African empire. The Portuguese, even less than other colonial powers, had no place in their colonial thinking for measures which might lead to the eventual independence of the Africans under their domination. Instead the Portuguese envisaged the assimilation of their subjects into a greater Portuguese state with equal rights for all individuals who accepted Portuguese culture and who, above all, were able to utilize the Portuguese language. But Portuguese metropolitan colonial theory was even farther removed from the reality of their African experience than the policies of the other principal European colonial powers. This very small and poor European nation did not possess the resources necessary for the massive and expensive educational effort required to give the Portuguese theory any chance of a successful culmination. Indeed the policy really was never attempted because of Portugal's weakness. In 1950, for example, there were only about 36,000 assimilated Africans included in the 10,500,000 inhabitants of Moçambique, Angola, and Guinea.

Moreover the sincerity of the Portuguese doctrine of assimilation was open to considerable doubt because of their treatment of the few Africans who did manage to overcome all of the obstacles to gaining a Portuguese education. The Portuguese boasted loudly of the nonracist character of their rule, but even the limited number of Africans who capped their careers by university training in Portugal discovered few openings for the use of their talents in Portugal's African world. The unassimilated majority of Portugal's African subjects were governed through a system of direct administration. Portuguese citizens were used even in the subordinate positions of the administering staff which other colonial powers usually left for Africans. Some traditional leaders, however, were given positions in the lower ranks. Unfortunately, Portuguese treatment of their African subjects was replete with abuses, especially in the use of forced labor, for the overwhelming mass of the populations left untouched by the doctrine so grandly enunciated by Portuguese colonial thinkers.

Britain and South Africa

In the European-settled regions of South Africa, which became a self-governing territory within the British Empire in the early twentieth century, the black inhabitants were destined to receive the harshest treatment given to Africans in all of the white-dominated regions of the continent. The long and difficult effort by the British to control the white Afrikaans-speaking peoples of the South had become increasingly troublesome following the great changes brought to these once economically backward regions by the discovery of diamonds in 1867 and of gold in 1886. The subsequent influx of a multinational horde of fortune seekers into the Afrikaner regions threatened to shake the control of the limited Afrikaner population—which numbered about 70,000 by the 1870s—of its own affairs in the interior republics of the Orange Free State and the Transvaal. Equally disruptive was the influence of the large capitalistic concerns which grew to dominate the mining industry. The Afrikaner position also was eroded increasingly by the policies of one of Britain's great imperial figures of the latter nineteenth century, Cecil Rhodes. Coming to South Africa in 1870 at the age of eighteen for reasons of health, Rhodes rose to dominate the diamond industry of the region through his company, De Beers Consolidated Mines, Ltd.; he later developed a similarly important position in the gold mining industry of the region through his Consolidated Gold Fields of South Africa, Ltd. Rhodes capped his local career by becoming prime minister of the self-governing Cape Colony in 1890. With his massive wealth, and his dream of a great British-dominated region in the southern section of the continent, Rhodes obviously was a dangerous threat to the Afrikaner way of life. But the equally determined leader of the Afrikaner people, President Paul Kruger of the Transvaal resolutely opposed any measures leading to his group's loss of the direction of their own destinies.

The many issues of increasing conflict, especially the ridiculously abortive 1895 raid of Leander Jameson into the Transvaal, which led to Rhodes' resignation as prime minister of the Cape Colony, culminated in the Boer War of 1899-1902. The British were required to fight a major colonial war before the defeat of the Afrikaners was accomplished. In their desperate effort for victory the British utilized many harsh techniques, including a scorched-earth policy and the creation of concentration camps for noncombatant populations, before the stubborn white defenders accepted defeat in the Treaty of Vereeniging. But once victory was achieved, the British were concerned to overcome the bitterness left by the war. They wished to see all of the polities of the southern continent united in one state that would cease to be a threat, through its continuing instability, to the strategic British position on the sea route to India. When British-inspired policies, directed until 1905 by the imperious Lord Milner, did not produce this unity but rather stimulated Afrikaner nationalism, the colonial masters left the resolution of the problem to the local white communities. As a result, the Orange Free State was given responsible government in 1906 and the Transvaal in 1907. After vigorous debates between the various South African European communities, the colonies of Natal, Cape Colony, Orange Free State, and the Transvaal were incorporated under a new constitution of 1910 into a single self-governing dominion, the Union of South Africa. The fears and aspirations of the black inhabitants of these areas were of little interest to either Briton or Boer during the deliberations. They were abandoned to the mercies of the rulers of the new British dominion, along with the Indian population of the region (one of whose leaders was then the young lawyer, Mahatma Gandhi), by a satisfied British government which hoped at last to have achieved the goal of a viable South Africa. It was one of the greatest betrayals of the trust that British theorists of their empire stressed as one of the main reasons for their presence in Africa.

Conclusions

The differences in the colonial ruling techniques of the various European nations with African dependencies probably are of more interest to the historian than to those Africans who had to endure the daily degradation of an alien rule. The techniques may have differed, and the amount of misrule and exploitation may have varied at different times in different colonies, but one underlying principle controlled the relationship everywhere between African and European. By the outbreak of World War I all of the indigenous inhabitants of the continent, except those in Ethiopia, had been deprived of the right to manage their own affairs in the political society of their birth or choice. Reduced to the status of colonial subjects, and often ruled by masters with pronounced racist attitudes, Africans suffered the supreme humiliation of being told by outsiders what components of their own cultures should be allowed to continue. This psychological exploitation must certainly be one of the most onerous aspects of colonialism. As one freedom-loving Tanzanian lamented in 1953: "To be governed by others. . . is shameful impotence."

7. Saadani Abu Kandoro, quoted in Andrew Maguire, "The Emergence of the Tanganyika African National Union in the Lake Province," in Robert I. Rotberg and Ali A. Mazrui, eds., *Power and Protest in Black Africa* (New York, 1970), p. 656.

5 African Responses

The nature of European colonial policies was influenced everywhere by the African reactions to the systems imposed upon them. The form of African resistance varied greatly in different regions of the continent, and even within the same colonial territory. One of the main foci of contemporary scholarship relating to Africa is the effort to understand and evaluate these hitherto little comprehended reactions. We have previously discussed some of the initial African resistance during the beginning period of colonial rule. The following section includes examples of the relationships between Africans and Europeans after the primary European conquest was completed, when Africans were being subjected to the ruling policies of their particular colonial masters.

African Rebellions

One of the most striking examples of African resistance to policies imposed without prior consultation, the Maji Maji Rebellion, occurred in German East Africa during the first decade of the twentieth century. The German government, which in 1891 had replaced the German East African Company's administration with direct imperial rule, had spent much of the 1890s in bringing their subjects under firm control. The process required major military actions against such important peoples as the Hehe, Chagga, and Nyamwezi. The government then considered itself ready to concentrate upon the major problems of securing the successful economic development of its East African possession. Since German East Africa contained no significant mineral wealth the source of any immediate progress was clearly centered in new agricultural experiments. Major research efforts were carried through by the methodical Germans to determine which crops should be encouraged. One important result was the successful beginning of the cultivation of sisal, a North American plant utilized in the making of fiber.

Another important experiment in this development planning was a policy designed to stimulate the cultivation and marketing of cotton. African farmers of the southern coastal regions, and a few nearby areas, were compelled from 1902 to concentrate their agricultural labors upon the growing of cotton in selected plots. This enforced measure became very unpopular, particularly when the Africans involved discovered to their dismay that the lack of success for the total scheme gave them virtually no financial return. They also suffered when their labors with cotton caused them to neglect the normal products of their subsistence agricultural patterns. Opposition turned to outright rebellion in July 1905 when the Matumbi and later other Africans of the region behind Kilwa rose to drive away the officials of the German administration. It was an unexpected uprising since this area of German East Africa was the homeland of African peoples with loosely structured political systems who never had been known for martial endeavors. The movement also spread to some neighboring territories; the warlike Ngoni, for example, joined the rebel cause. There was an important religious underpinning to the African resistance. The movement took its name from the ritual use of water, *maji* in the Swahili language, to give protection from the firearms of the Europeans. The use of the *maji* also importantly provided a commitment to one's comrades in the resistance. Initially the *maji* was distributed by the priest of the Bokero (or Kolelo) cult. Eventually, after the first African defeats, the *maji* became linked to a belief among some of the participating Africans in the arrival of a better future world.

The Germans feared the consequences of the uprising upon their yet unsteady colonial structure, especially if many of the previously conquered peoples of German East Africa decided to join the ranks of Maji Maji. Thus they reacted quickly and harshly to crush the dissident Africans. With their superior military resources, and aided by the failure of the uprising to spread to most of their colony, the Germans were able by August 1905 to break the forward impetus of the rebels. Resistance among a few African peoples, however, was maintained until early 1907. The Africans of the participating societies suffered heavily from the German repression. Implicated leaders of the rebels were summarily "tried" and executed. A famine also followed the hostilities, significantly increasing the loss of life. In all, the total African loss from Maji Maji and its consequences has been estimated at about 75,000 individuals. The relatively underdeveloped southern region of the future Tanzania had suffered a major blow to its efforts to achieve prosperous growth.

Nonetheless the Maji Maji Rebellion had significant implications for the future. When Tanzanians after World War II organized in their movement to gain independence, the rebellion against the German rulers was given special significance. In it, for the first time, Africans from many diverse tribal groupings had submerged their particularist views to unite against a common oppressor. In Tanzanian history the Maji Maji Rebellion justly can be regarded as the incipient beginning of a modern nationalism. More immediately, the hostilities had an important influence upon the evolution of German colonial policy for their East African territory. The new governor of German East Africa, Albrecht von Rechenberg, made it a cardinal point of his subsequent policies not to subvert unduly African customs and aspirations in ways which might lead to another unwanted and costly uprising. Von Rechenberg also had initial support from another consequence of the Maji Maji Rebellion, an independent German colonial office under the direction of the first colonial secretary, Bernhard von Dernburg. During his term of office in East Africa (1906-12), the talented von

Rechenberg pushed through a series of policies designed to better the future of Africans. They included measures giving protection from excessive mistreatment from German officials and settlers, as well as new ventures to stimulate African agriculture to make it a main source of the colony's revenues. A primary component of the agricultural development schemes was von Rechenberg's decision to construct a railroad connecting the coastal capital, Dar es Salaam, to Tabora in the center of the colony, and to Kigoma on Lake Tanganyika. The railroad was designed to allow the industrious African agriculturalists of the central regions, especially the Nyamwezi and Sukuma peoples, a profitable outlet for their products. The existing system of human porterage, which hitherto had been necessary for all transport, had by its heavy unit costs precluded the movement of any but luxury products to the coast. Unfortunately for the Germans, however, the railroad to Kigoma was not completed until 1914, thus leaving the full benefits of the costly undertaking to the new British rulers of the colony. Von Rechenberg also endeavored to prevent the growing German settler community from gaining too important a place within the territory. This policy of the governor was not so successful since the settlers, through their influence in the German metropolitan legislature (which ultimately controlled colonial administration), were able to counter von Rechenberg's aspirations. Nevertheless von Rechenberg had provided the African subjects he governed with a sound and fair administration, one as favorable to their interests as perhaps any alien colonial structure could be. And the stirring events of the Maji Maji Rebellion, which had demonstrated what an aroused and partially united African mass movement could accomplish, were a major determinant in settling the German governor onto his chosen course of colonial policy.

An equally important African uprising against a colonial administration occurred in the 1890s in the British territory of Southern Rhodesia. This region had been occupied by the third of the British chartered companies operating in Africa, the British South Africa Company of Cecil Rhodes, founded in 1889. In his drive to extend British territory to the north of the unfriendly Afrikaner states, Rhodes had established his followers in the territories of the Ndebele and Shona peoples by 1890. Permanent settlers were included among the early arrivals, thus insuring them a role in government from the beginning of the company's administation. This advantage made them a considerably more formidable group than the settlers in other British areas—like Kenya—who arrived only after company or official rule had commenced. With Rhodes' large financial resources available to buttress the European occupation—a railroad, for example, connected them to the European-dominated regions of the south by 1897—the settlers early held a very commanding position vis-a-vis the African inhabitants. The martial Ndebele, under their astute warrior-leader, Lobengula, had been defeated by the new arrivals in 1893 as the result of a campaign which the Europeans, conscious of their strength, had forced upon the Africans. The loss cost the Ndebele much of their best land and a large portion of their treasured cattle herds. The more peaceful Shona-speaking peoples, who were until the European victory subordinate to the Ndebele, consequently became subject to an increasing European infiltration.

The British Colonial Office left the administration of the newly conquered territory to Rhodes's company. Although a Native Comissioner was appointed in 1894, that official did little to mitigate the sufferings the Africans experienced at the hands of their conquerers. They instead were subject to abuses from the administration in the form of an unchecked collection of a hut tax—often through raiding—and the enforcement of harsh policies designed to secure African labor for the settlers. These were dangerous proceedings, however: in the face of European overconfidence in their military prowess, the African populations still possessed considerable powers of resistance.

The continuing European exactions against Ndebele land and cattle, coupled with a rinderpest epidemic which struck heavily at the remaining herds, drove the desperate people to rebellion in March 1896. A major difference from the earlier hostilities was that the Shona, who did not join in the 1893 war between the British and the Ndebele, also took up arms, a circumstance which completely surprised the settlers. The Shona had acted because of factors influencing their own society alone, not because of any alliance with the Ndebele. The most important stimulation to the Shona was a serious lack of rainfall which had convinced them that the Europeans had not properly paid heed to the gods of their region. Neither African people had a unified political leadership to direct their war effort. The Ndebele system had split into fractions following the disappearance of Lobengula after the 1893 campaign, while the Shona never had possessed centralized institutions. But as in the Maji Maji rising, religious leaders emerged to help in supplying effective direction.

When the British South Africa Company proved unable to suppress the rebellion, partly because its forces had been weakened by their participation in the abortive Jameson Raid on the Transvaal, the British government intervened with its military forces. The move was dangerous for Rhodes, then unpopular in Britain because of his involvement in the Jameson Raid, causing him to take dramatic action to quicken the war's end. In 1896 Rhodes sought out the Ndebele leaders, meeting with them in negotiations which led some Africans to conclude peace in return for certain advantages, including positions within the colony's Native Authority. The lesser Ndebele chiefs and the religious leaders, however, were left open to punishment. The Shona, not a participant in the negotiations for surrender, struggled on until the end of 1897. Imperial force was used against them, including the dynamiting of caves serving as bases for their resistance. The Shona fighting ability was maintained by the effectiveness of their religious leaders, but the British pressure was unceasing. The last two spirit mediums, Kagubi and Nehanda, were taken in the last months of 1897; they were executed during the following April.

The events of this hard war had important influences upon the development of future British policy in Southern Rhodesia which were not so sanguine for Africans as the post-Maji Maji policies in German East Africa. The hostilities had left ample indication of the potential disorder that outraged Africans could create. Consequently the Native Authority was reorganized to eliminate the unchecked excesses of the past. The settlers profited from the events of the war. Nevertheless they were extremely bitter at the policies of the British South Africa Company; they blamed it for the rising which had cost the settler community one-tenth of its population. This hostility was an important factor for Rhodes to consider. The territory administered by his company was dependent upon the settlers both for economic progress and military support. To counter their anger

Rhodes successfully won their support with an offer of settler representation in government, given with a clear implication that self-government awaited them in the future.

Meantime the British government had become increasingly disenchanted with the problems caused by chartered companies. It threw its support to the settlers as a balancing force to Rhodes' position. Rhodes died in 1902. The Colonial Office also considered that the settlers would provide a better government for the territory, and more importantly, it wanted to ensure that if Rhodes' company was replaced the local government would be able to assume the financial responsibilities for the colony. In October 1898 a legislative council, with four representatives of the settler community, was created; it gained a settler majority in 1908. The move toward full European control was underway. It was achieved in 1923 when Britain, following a settler vote in favor of self-government and against incorporation in the Union of South Africa, ended the chartered company's political role and annexed the territory. The African majority was relegated to the background; the Shona suffered from the total dislocation of their society resulting from the 1896 war, while the Ndebele gradually lost the few advantages their early surrender had gained.

There were numerous other instances during the early period of colonial administration of martial reactions by Africans to European policies. Many, however, were little heard of outside Africa since they often occurred among the smaller African societies located in regions in hard to reach interior areas.[1] But the overwhelming military strength of the Europeans made defeat, plus the subsequent measures of

1. See, for example, the many instances documented in G. H. Mungeam, *British Rule in Kenya, 1895-1912* (Oxford, 1966).

punishment, too evident for Africans to undertake an open resistance unless ·an overwhelming sense of oppression and despair overrode all of the consequences of European victory. Africans instead had to endure foreign rule with an outward calm acceptance, meanwhile preparing themselves or their children to be ready for any future opportunities to secure freedom from alien control. Only one practicable way was open for attaining that goal: the participation by Africans in the educational processess brought by their rulers. In this manner they might share in the knowledge of the techniques which had allowed Europeans to dominate the world.

Africans and Western Education

A few Africans had had the opportunity to acquire a formal Western education from virtually the earliest period of the modern European presence in their continent. The impact upon their own societies of this small band of individuals, who were mostly drawn from the areas of the European trading settlments along the West African coast, had been minimal, although some individuals did secure prestige and profit for themselves and their descendants. More opportunities for African education became available from the close of the eighteenth century, because a resurgence of Christian vitality in Europe quickly made the dispatching of missionaries to non-Christian lands a central part of religious activity. Among British groups the Baptist Missionary Society, the London Missionary Society, and the Church Missionary Society, were founded respectively in 1792, 1795, and 1799. The many non-British organizations included the American Board of Commissioners to Foreign Missions (1810) and the Paris Evangelical Society (1828). Roman Catholicism was somewhat slower in revivifying its former missionary zeal in Africa, but it too, particularly among French Catholics, became increasingly active. Missionary societies taught Africans for their own religious aims, of course, and by their own particular methods, and consequently only a very small elite ever was able to progress to the higher grades of education. In British-dominated regions the course of African educational progress was concentrated overwhelmingly in the coastal belt of West Africa, in Sierra Leone—where Fourah Bay College was founded in 1827—the Gold Coast, and Nigeria. English-speaking Liberia also participated in this development; its educational system was capped by the foundation of the University of Liberia in 1862. In French-dominated Africa there was little opportunity for significant indigenous higher education, even in Senegal, until the twentieth century.

An example of what a Western-educated African could achieve during the early period of the modern European presence is demonstrated in the career of Samuel Adjai Crowther. Of Yoruba origin, Crowther had been captured during the Yoruba wars of the 1820s and sold to Portuguese slavers. After being rescued at sea by the Royal Navy, Crowther was brought to the freed slave settlement of Sierra Leone. Entering the schools run by the Church Missionary Society, he gained both an education and the Christian religion. Crowther was sent to Britain in 1826 for further education; he returned to Sierra Leone in 1827 to become one of the first. African students at the recently founded institution at Fourah Bay. The young African convert was ordained a Christian minister in 1843. In the 1850s he accompanied a pioneering British venture up the Niger, and in 1864 Crowther became the first black Anglican bishop. Thereafter he had a career of great distinction in the missionary field in Nigeria, a career unfortunately marred near the end of his life (in 1891) by the rising flood of European racism. Nevertheless, to the Western world, Crowther was one of the most famous of nineteenth-century Africans; his impact upon aspiring young Africans who lived in societies held under the British domination was also considerable.

There were no equivalent patterns for the spread of Western education in nineteenth-century East Africa. Effective missionary activity was slow in emerging in this region, dating from the arrival of the French Holy Ghost Fathers and the British Universities' Mission to Central Africa in Zanzibar in 1860 and 1864 respectively. The few Western-educated Africans of this period before the European partition were typified by the example of the Yao William Jones. Rescued from an Arab slaver by a Royal Navy vessel, the young Jones was sent to India where he received a basic education at British missionary hands. Returning to East Africa he entered the service of the Church Missionary Society as a teacher at their Mombasa station, the old center of Krapf, Rebmann, and Erhardt, which had been revivified in the 1870s. Jones did, through his considerable talents, gain an impressive local reputation, but he remained until his death a subordinate worker in a British-directed system. Other Africans with backgrounds roughly similar to that of Jones made their way in East African careers which were not always centered around the European missionary societies. Such was the career of Jacob Wainwright, a liberated slave of Central African origins. Sent from a British institution in India to serve on Livingstone's last expedition, Wainwright gave the Scots missionary-explorer faithful service until his death. Wainwright was one of the Africans who returned Livingstone's remains to Zanzibar and subseqently he traveled to London to serve as one of the two African pallbearers at the explorer's Westminster Abbey funeral. Returning to East Africa, where he often twitted Britons by saying that he had been received by Queen Victoria while they had not, Wainwright held a variety of positions under missionary and other European employers. But Wainwright never was to achieve any substantial position in the increasingly European-dominated world of East Africa. He died in the African interior as an almost forgotten figure. It was only toward the close of the nineteenth century that the Zanzibar educational establishment of the Universities' Mission to Central Africa began to graduate a growing number of Western-educated churchmen and teachers. By 1911 almost 600 Africans had received an education there. Many of the graduates soon left the service of the mission to provide some of the earliest educated manpower for the East African private sector. But by that time European rule had begun in East Africa and the racism which had blighted Bishop Crowther's later years similarly kept these Africans in subordinate, albeit important, positions within that region's society.

Once European colonial administration began to function, schools became a vital necessity for the training of Africans in order to qualify them for the many subordinate positions required in a colonial state. The pioneers of Western education, the missionaries, continued to hold a prominent position in the colonial era since they possessed experienced personnel and because the utilization of their teachers and buildings resulted in a considerable financial saving in the usually sparse colonial budgets. In Nigeria, for example, the missions controlled 99% of the schools and enrolled 97% of the pupils in the country in 1942. But such statistics covered only a very limited fraction of the school-age population. In 1939 in Nigeria only 12% of those eligible were in schools. And in 1942 there were less than 2,000 pupils in Nigeria's secondary schools. In addition these schools did not provide a free education as was the case in similar Belgian and French institutions. One important reason for the limited number of pupils was the failure of the metropolitan governments to formulate an effective educational policy for their colonies. The British, for example, did not evolve a formal statement for an imperial policy of education until 1925 when their government provided grants to missionary schools. Significant imperial financial aid did not come until after 1940. Thus if a colony or a region, such as Northern Nigeria, did not divert local resources to education, or did not have missionary institutions, there was little modern education. As a consequence, in 1951 only one individual out of the 16,000,000 indigenous inhabitants of Northern Nigeria possessed a university degree.

Colonial governments, however, did not leave the educational sector entirely to missionaries. In some European states, notably France, many citizens were opposed to the participation of religious organizations in education. In the early twentieth century France ended state subsidies for religious schools, but nevertheless they continued to hold a favored position within the French system. In 1938, for example, there were 70,000 children in schools, about 20% of them under missionary aegis, in French West Africa. In other colonial areas mission schools, especially those of fundamentalist Protestant sects, often did not follow curricula that most suited the secular needs of local governments. Thus, for example, the Germans opened a government-run school at Tanga in 1893; by 1903 there were eight such schools in German East Africa. In Uganda in 1922 a school for carpentry and mechanics was inaugurated at Makerere by the government; later expansion there took place along vocational lines and in teacher training.

Opportunities for Africans in higher education were extremely limited until very late in the colonial period. French policies of education, which required the use of the French language by pupils in the primary schools, added to the fact that little of their various colonies' resources were expended in education, insured the training of a very numerically limited elite. Local institutions, such as the Ecole Normale William Ponty near Dakar, trained Africans for positions in teaching and government, but these schools were very few. The few Africans going on to university work were educated in France since there were no universities in French Africa until after World War II. The British had several institutions of higher learning within Africa. Fourah Bay College in Sierra Leone was founded by the Church Missionary Society; in 1876 it became a university college affiliated with Durham University. The major development of universities in British Africa followed World War II, when institutions were established in many colonies.

Africans themselves also took matters of education into their own hands when they considered that the colonial governments were not doing an adequate job. In 1924, for example, the government of Kenya devoted only 4% of its revenues to education, while Uganda and Tanganyika spent 2% and 1% respectively. As a reaction the Kikuyu of Kenya, who had evolved a strong feeling for their own development during the period between the two world wars, founded their own churches and schools, including the important Kikuyu Independent Schools Association. By this means they allowed many additional African individuals to be prepared to profit from the opportunities opened by the requirements of the colonial system.

Little is yet known of the Western-educated Africans of the early colonial period, an era which a British scholar has aptly characterized as "the age of improvement and differentiation."[2] They were the first Africans educated to carry on important functions for their colonial rulers. They were sorely needed. In 1914, for example, the Germans in their East African territory had only seventy-nine European administrators to rule a country with a population of about 4,000,000 spread out over about 400,000 square miles. The subordinate African officials perforce accepted the dominance of their colonial rulers. Even if these Africans possessed the disposition to oppose them, the failure of the early resistance efforts had demonstrated the futility of military solutions. If there was to be continuing resistance, it appeared far more useful to do it by working within the colonial system, by slanting the information upon which decisions of colonial policy were based to the advantage of Africans, or by influencing the manner in which regulations were enforced upon Africans once the policy decisions had been made. And of course in the colonial territories where many languages were spoken, the European rulers were largely dependent for administrative details upon the accuracy of the translations given them by African subordinates. But perhaps the most important influence of the

2. See John Iliffe, "The Age of Improvement and Differentiation (1907-45)," in I. N. Kimambo and A. J. Temu. eds., *A History of Tanzania* (Nariobi, 1969), pp. 123-60.

early African officials was their impact upon the future evolution of the colonial relationship. Knowing full well the value of Western education, the African officials made sure that their sons and other relatives gained the knowledge necessary for their advancement. And these young men, growing up with the awareness of the opportunities offered by the educational systems of their rulers, were often prepared once their first schooling was accomplished to seek higher degrees. They were also a living example to ambitious young Africans from traditional homes. They saw that if they wanted to rise in their own societies, and of even more importance, that if they wished to understand the European-dominated world around them, that the path of the future was through Western education.

Other Africans rose within the colonial system through the expanded economic opportunities open to them. The cocoa of the Africans of the Gold Coast, or the cotton of the Sukuma of Tanganyika, brought sufficient profit to individuals, who often acted through associations of growers, to allow them to build for the future. And in the growing urban centers of colonial Africa rural Africans, often far from their kinsmen, formed many associations to allow them to master, or at least to survive, their changed environments. The cities, in fact, were vital centers for the development of African nationalism, where rural Africans passed from the rules of their tribal systems to those of a newly emerging African world. Trade unions, for example, were not long in forming; the first major strike in Tanganyika happened in 1937 among the dockworkers of Tanga.[3]

It was from the young men of both these backgrounds, influenced by either the formal educational system of the rulers

3. For an interesting account of the trade union movement, see the novel *God's Bits of Wood* by Ousmane Sembène (Garden City, N. Y., 1970).

or by the institutions that these rulers had brought to their countries, that many of the leaders of Africa's struggle for independence came. Léopold Sédar Senghor, the son of a rich merchant family, and Julius Nyerere, the son of a minor traditional ruler, the present leaders of Senegal and Tanzania, are products of the new educated generation, while Sékou Touré, the ruler of Guinée, rose from the ranks of trade unions.

Further African resistance to their European-dominated societies occurred in the religious sphere through separatist movements or chiliastic sects. Examples of movements which evolved free of European control were the African Watchtower (Kitawala) group of Central Africa, or the United Native African Church in Nigeria. In the Congo an African prophet, Simon Kimbangu, emerged in 1921 to spread his version of the Gospel. Although he neither denounced Europeans nor attempted to found his own church, Kimbangu's movement grew. Others soon exploited it to stimulate disobedience to the Belgian government of the Congo. Kimbangu was arrested, convicted of treason and sedition, and, after his death sentence was commuted, was sentenced to life imprisonment. He died in prison in 1951, but the movement he inspired has continued. Such movements gave Africans, who had been denied the equality inherent in Western Christianity, the opportunity to achieve positions of responsibility in their own organizations, and thus to better prepare themselves for a future free from foreign domination.

Early Nationalist Movements

The beginnings of modern nationalism within Africa

probably first emerged among the various North African populations and among the African-born whites of South Africa. It previously has been explained how the Dutch and other settlers of the South had slowly developed their own language and African way of life. And although the Afrikaners had been defeated in battle by their British sovereigns during the Boer War, both settler communities of Boer and Briton had united peacefully in 1910 to gain internal self-government, from that time forth to consciously advance policies designed to maintain the black majority of South Africans in apparently perpetual servitude.

The North Africans set a far different example, establishing broad patterns in their slow development of nationalism which were often repeated at later dates in most of Europe's African colonies. During the nineteenth century many of the significant thinkers of the Islamic world had begun analyzing why their Muslim societies had lost their vitality and why their individual countries had either fallen outright to European conquerers or had become subject to overriding European political and economic influence. Thus individuals like the Egyptian scholar Muhammad Abduh, or the writer Jamal al-Din al-Afghani, began seeking a method to accomodate their Islamic culture to the contemporary developments of the secular Western technology while yet maintaining the spiritual force of their Muslim religion. It was a difficult task since the reformers were opposed by the traditional upholders of Muslim thought and hampered by the formidable problems of transmitting their message to the largely uneducated masses of their territories who normally looked to the traditional leaders for guidance.

The first outstanding manifestations of these heady dogmas of reform came in Egypt where the many modernizing schemes of the dynasty founded by Muhammad Ali had undermined the financial strength of the country. During the rule of Said (1854-63), the Frenchman Ferdinand de Lesseps gained a concession for a canal to connect the Red Sea to the Mediterranean. The actual construction of the canal did not start until the reign of Said's successor, Ismail, began in 1863. The Suez Canal was opened in 1869, but it had proved a costly venture for the Egyptians; they had paid all but £4,500,000 of the estimated £16,000,000 cost of construction. This heavy burden, added to the debts caused by many of Ismail's other modernizing efforts, caused financial difficulties for the Egyptian government, allowing the astute Benjamin Disraeli to buy the Egyptian shares in the canal for the British government at a price of £4,000,000. But Egypt's debts continued to mount, reaching by 1876 a total of about £100,000,000. In that year Ismail had to suspend payment on the national debt and, following negotiations with Egypt's creditors, to accept an international supervisory commission to administer the financial system of his country. When Ismail attempted to challenge this control in 1879 he was deposed, with his son Tawfiq being appointed in his place.

The change of rulers, however, did not end the ferment within Egypt. Egyptians after all had been studying many of the aspects of western civilization since the early days of the century when Muhammad Ali had begun the modernization of his adopted country. By the 1880s a group of radical reformers, centered in the Egyptian army, coalesced behind Ahmad Arabi to seek measures allowing Egyptians to regain control of their country's policies. The inadequately educated military men had a limited following among the other liberal leaders of that era and especially among the masses of the indigenous population. Nevertheless they were powerful enough within the narrow governing circles to successfully gain control of the administration of Egypt, to depose Tawfiq, and to work for reforms which the involved European nations considered detrimental to their interests. After the growing internal tension erupted into rioting against Europeans at Alexandria and other locations, the British, driven by their worry over the security of the Suez Canal, decided to intervene. The Egyptians resisted the invaders, but they were no match for their superior military organization. The Egyptian army was crushed at al-Tal al-Kabir in 1882. Arabi and other leaders were exiled to Ceylon, and under the restored Tawfiq the administration of Egypt was effectively controlled by the occupying British conquerers. Their lasting intervention in Egyptian internal affairs did not end until 1956, although nationalistic pressures were continuously projected against the British from the beginning of the twentieth century by such leaders as Mustafa Kamil, Muhammad Farid, and Saad Zaghlul. To further their policy goals Britain in 1922 granted a limited internal independence to Egypt, reserving for itself significant powers over the control of the Suez Canal, national defense, protection of foreigners, and the administration of the Anglo-Egyptian Sudan. Thus the continuing evolution of Egypt to full independence after World War II followed a course not typical of other Egyptian-dominated African lands.

Tunisia, like Egypt a country with a long continuity of development as a separate political entity, underwent a similar, although less spectacular, attempt at modernization during the nineteenth century. And, as in Egypt, the heavy debts created by an inefficient government led to bankruptcy. Thus in 1869 the control of the financial administration of

Tunisia was given to an international commission. Though the Tunisians avoided an outright challenge on the Egyptian model to the concerned European powers, they nevertheless were one of the first African countries to fall under European rule during the 1880s. Tunisian independence ended before the naked expansionism of the policies of French premier Jules Ferry. The forms of the independent Tunisian government were maintained under a French protectorate, but the essential direction of policy passed to the invaders.

The Tunisians, however, had inaugurated modern educational reform before the French conquest; the important Sadiqi College was founded in 1875. Steps toward the evolution of a more efficient traditional education came with the creation of the Khalduniya school in 1895, the result of an earlier visit of the Islamic reformer Muhammad Abduh to Tunisia. Consequently, by World War II, there was present a class of educated young men ready to begin reacting against their colonial rulers and the tensions of an increasing French presence which then numbered 240,000. One organization, the Young Tunisians, many of whom were alumni of Sadiqi College, was created in 1905. They organized to achieve equal opportunities of participation for Muslims in the social and economic life of the protectorate; they realistically gave less emphasis to political advancement. But although a modern nationalism, with roots in the masses of the population, was slow in developing, by 1911 the feeling of unease among Tunisians was acute enough to lead to riots against the French for their interference with a Muslim graveyard. It was still too early, however, for an effective union among Tunisians of all classes against their foreign rulers.

In Tunisia, as in the rest of Africa, the most dramatic advances in the early development of nationalism followed the European catastrophe of World War I. Before the war most of the protests motivated by modernizing ideas necessarily remained very limited in scope. Additional time was required for the spread of the new forces brought to Africa by the European conquest before new forms of opposition could become effective. After World War I, Woodrow Wilson's Fourteen Points were known to many literate Africans, who hoped to see them applied to the peoples of their continent.[4] Equally important were the varied experiences of the numerous Africans of all social classes who had served in Europe as members of the military forces of their colonial rulers. The French in particular made extensive use of men from all parts of Africa; about 200,000 Africans were recruited during the war years from French West Africa alone. The enlarging of the intellectual horizons of these African veterans through their direct experience of the merits and demerits of European civilization as practiced in its home areas necessarily influenced their conduct when they returned to their subordinate positions in the African colonies.

But any aspirations for immediate major improvments in the colonial relationship remained unsatisfied. When the victorious Allies concluded the Treaty of Versailles with Germany and its supporters, the Fourteen Points were not applied to African territories. Instead the mandate system of

4. The fifth point read: "A free, open-minded, and absolutely impartial adjustment of all colonial claims, based upon a strict observance of the principle that in determining all such questions of sovereignty the interests of the populations concerned must have equal weight with the equitable claims of the government whose title is to be determined." Quoted in Ruhl J. Bartlett, *The Record of American Diplomacy*, 4th ed. (New York, 1964), p. 460.

the League of Nations served as a convenient expedient to allow the victors to retain the spoils of battle. Some Africans, allied with individuals of African descent from the New World, did attempt to influence the negotiations through a Pan-African conference held in Paris in 1919, but they were unable to exert any effective political impact. Africans had to continue with a basic acceptance of the colonial system while building their strength in the face of an uncertain future through participation in Western education and incipient political organizations. Postwar events did, however, demonstrate that world opinion toward dependent territories perhaps was changing. The creation of the Irish Free State in 1921, Egypt's limited independence of 1922, the rise of the Indian Congress Party, and the Statute of Westminster of 1931 establishing the British Commonwealth were all watched from Africa.

Nevertheless most politically active Africans, whatever their personal aspirations resulting from the war-influenced events, did not seriously think of any effort to expel their European rulers by force. In French Africa, for example, the vitality of the assimilationist tendency of French colonial policy was demonstrated through the career of the Senegalese politician Blaise Diagne. As discussed earlier, Diagne took advantage of France's wartime requirement for African manpower to gain the reconfirmation of the rights of French citizenship for the inhabitants of Senegal's four communes. The *Loi Diagne* of 1916 achieved this goal for the inhabitants and their descendants, while allowing them to retain the jurisdiction of their family law. Disputes over civil status, however, continued until 1932, when a decree was issued limiting the authority of the rules of Muslim law to personal matters. Many of the other wartime promises made to Diagne by the French government were not kept. Nevertheless, after the war's end, Diagne remained working within the French government, becoming increasingly more conservative and stressing the virtues of French colonial policy. He particularly advanced the opportunities it allowed—as seen in his career—for effective African participation within the French system. Diagne died in 1934, after a distinguished career, but many observers always justly commented that it was a most exceptional one. Other Africans, in humbler positions, whoever their colonial rulers, also generally labored for improvement within their respective systems. But they did so without Diagne's enthusiasm, simply accepting the realities of power in the world in which they lived.

The pace of African protest did increase greatly in the post-World War I years. In Kenya, for example, the largely missionary-run schools among the Kikuyu, the colony's largest African grouping, were producing a series of men ready to speak out against the injustices perpetrated upon Africans. In 1921 an organization called the Young Kikuyu Association became prominent. Its secretary was Harry Thuku, a man of some education, who had been a government telephone operator until his political activities caused his dismissal. He had spoken out against the *kipande,* a fingerprinted card required of Africans under a registration system, and against the increasing of the African hut tax. An indication of the future course of action of African leaders was Thuku's endeavor to extend his appeal beyond the boundaries of his own ethnic group, the Kikuyu. But it was too early in the colonial period for such political activity to be successful. A nervous Kenyan government, worried about Thuku's potential appeal, arrested the African politician in 1922, thereafter deporting him to a remote Somali town. One result of this government action was a major African riot in Nairobi. But there was no significant African follow-up, and the settler-dominated colony rested easily for a time.

When the British metropolitan government began to consider schemes leading to a potential union of its East African colonies, however, African opinon was once more heard. The Africans also became aroused by a missionary attack upon what they considered a vital Kikuyu custom, female circumcision. The major protest organization was the Kikuyu Central Association (KCA), the successor to Thuku's earlier group. The KCA possessed an energetic general secretary who was to dominate the future of Kenyan politics. Jomo Kenyatta, born Johnstone Kamau Ngengi in 1890, was the son of a Kikuyu agriculturalist. After receiving some education at a Church of Scotland mission school near Nairobi, Kenyatta entered government service as a minor official. The African opposition to European policies had created a need for potential leaders with a knowledge of the English language, and in 1928 Kenyatta became the general secretary of the KCA with the task of encouraging the spread of modern ideas of political growth among Kenya's Africans. Kenyatta began to acquire a national reputation when he testified in 1928 before the British commission investigating the idea of a closer union in East Africa. Then in 1929 Kenyatta was sent to Britain by the KCA to present to the Colonial Office an African point of view on Kenya's continuing land problem, as well as on several other issues. Actually, only a relatively small segment of Kikuyu land had been taken from them by the Europeans, about 109.5 square miles out of a total of 1,800 square miles, but the loss included some of the best of the agricultural land. More important, it became a pressing problem when the expanding Kikuyu population required additional territory. And the lost land always remained a political factor because the relationship to it of the Kikuyu was at the heart of their social system.

Following his not very successful testimony on the land problem, Kenyatta broadened his horizons by travel to Germany and the Soviet Union before returning to Kenya. In 1931 he was dispatched once more to Britain to present African opinion. This time the emerging African leader remained absent from his homeland for fifteen years. It was a significant absence. As part of the program of studies begun in Britain, Kenyatta entered the London School of Economics to work under the noted anthropologist Bronislaw Malinowski. The result was the 1938 publication of Kenyatta's *Facing Mount Kenya,* one of the earliest volumes by an African author which discussed his own culture without apology. Among other issues Kenyatta explained the relevance of female circumcision to the total culture of the Kikuyu, demonstrating how European observers had neglected this vital ritual aspect of an important African cultural facet. Fortunately for his future career, Kenyatta did not return to Kenya until after World War II. This proved imporant, since during the 1930s the strong European position within Kenya had blunted the African political emergence. African protest within Kenya through legal organizations increasingly became an exercise in political futility. The resulting frustration among African leaders led to personal quarrels which reduced what little chance the Africans had of making any political impact. But whatever the outward results of these beginning stages of modern political protest in Kenya, the experiences gained in the initial efforts in organizations directed against the colonial rulers at least had continued the traditions of African resistance, leaving a residue of knowledge and personal experience for use in the new era opening in Kenya after World War II.

Roughly similar happenings were occurring elsewhere in Africa. In France's Algerian territory, for example, early nationalist voices were heard. In Algeria where the European settler minority had exercised dominating influence since the latter part of the nineteenth century, several special characteristics, including the close social, economic, and political ties between France and Algeria, stimulated the aspirations of the Muslim Algerians. One group of individuals, whose most prominent representative was Farhat Abbas, pursued the assimilationist dream of French colonial theory. From the late 1920s Abbas steadfastly affirmed that France had much to offer the Muslim Algerians. Already assimilated themselves to the sometimes hidden democratic roots of French society, Abbas and his colleagues wished to see formed an amalgam of the best elements of French and Algerian cultures. Rejecting a separate Algerian development, Abbas during the 1930s movingly asserted: "If I had discovered the Algerian nation I would be a nationalist and would not blush as if it were a crime. . . . But I will not die for an Algerian fatherland because that fatherland does not exist, I have not discovered it. I have asked history, I have asked the living and the dead: I have visited the cemeteries; no one has spoken to me of it. . . ."[5] However impracticable future events made this attitude appear, it was then a

5. Quoted in Charles F. Gallagher, *The United States and North Africa* (Cambridge, 1963), p. 95.

worthwhile goal. But Muslim Algerians striving to achieve it were met at virtually every step by French Algerians who were determined not to allow the Muslims to gain any significant role in the determining of policy within their mutual homeland.

All Muslim Algerians did not share the views of the assimilationists. One group, led by the determined Messali al-Hajj, followed modern political paths, forming in the 1920s the first Algerian political party, the North African Star (Etoile Nord-Africaine). Drawing its membership from the many Algerian workers residing in France, the socialist-oriented organization clearly stood for the independence of Algeria and for the return to Muslim ownership of the lands then held by the French. The realities of that era, however, did not allow Messali al-Hajj's group to operate within Algeria, and thus it had little immediate impact. More important within the confines of the territory was the reaction of the more traditionalist Muslim Algerians. Directed by religious leaders, such as Abd al-Hamid ibn Badis, they rejected both the assimilationist thought of Abbas and the socialist tendencies of Messali al-Hajj in favor of a local evolution fixed firmly within the context of Muslim society. Ibn Badis answered Abbas's statement about the lack of an Algerian nation with these stirring words:

> History has taught us that the Muslim people of Algeria were created like all others. They have their history, illustrated by noble deeds; they have their religious unity and their language; they have their culture, their customs, their habits with all that is good and bad in them. This Muslim population is not France; it cannot be France, it does not want to be France. It is a population far from France in its language, its life and its religion; it does not seek to incor-

porate itself in France. It possesses its fatherland whose frontiers are fixed, and this is the Algerian fatherland.[6]

Despite the political vitality of the arguments between Muslim Algerians concerning the relationship with their French rulers, the colonial framework remained unshaken. The settlers and their metropolitan allies continued to be the directors of policy, defeating with their combined strength the Blum-Violette Bill in 1938, a proposal which had authorized some minor assimilationist steps. The defeat ended any hopes of significant assimilation for the pre-World War II period. All further developments affecting the future course of Algerian nationalism had to await the war's outcome.

Ending the Colonial Era

The shattering global conflict of World War II had a much greater impact upon colonial Africa than the 1914-18 war. In the Far East the Japanese quickly conquered the European possessions, vividly illustrating the fragile nature of European rule. In France the graceless collapse of the Third Republic led to the conflicting governments of Philippe Pétain and Charles de Gaulle, thus forcing the colonial administrators of France's African empire to chose one or the other as the legitimate government of France. Most of the colonial governors opted for Pétain's Vichy state, but in French Equatorial Africa the governor of the colony of Chad, Félix Eboué, a black from France's South American territory of Guyane, threw his support to de Gaulle's Free French

6. Quoted in Gallagher, *U. S. and North Africa*, p. 95.

government in exile. Eboué's decision provided de Gaulle with his first significant power base in French territory in his difficult campaign to be reconginzed as the legitimate leader of the French nation. And from the equatorial region a Free French military expedition led by Jacques Leclerc gave de Gaulle one of his first victories through a successful attack upon the Italians in Libya. Following the Allied landings in North Africa in 1943 French West Africa also declared for de Gaulle. Consequently de Gaulle and other Frenchmen were fully aware that changes in the African policy of France, reflecting the African support for the Free French war effort, had to follow the conflict's termination. Britain's colonial governments were not required to undergo a similar dramatic course. Nevertheless the colonies supplied important manpower, both black and white, and materials for campaigns ranging from Italy to Burma, as well as for the liberation of Ethiopia and the conquest of Somaliland from the Italians in speedy operations during 1941.

The propaganda machine organized for World War II by the Allied Powers was as significant in its colonial influences as the similar effort of World War I. The third clause of the Atlantic Charter, the result of a 1941 meeting between Winston S. Churchill and Franklin Delano Roosevelt, recalled Wilson's Fourteen Points and his campaign to make the world safe for democracy. The Charter of the United Nations, adopted by the Allies in 1945, further enshrined such principles as a people's right to the free determination of their own government. Equally important to some Africans was the presence of Allied troops in Africa. The American invaders of North Africa, with their tradition of hostility to other nations' rule, led North African nationalists to hope for postwar changes in the colonial structures of

Morocco, Algeria, Tunisia, and Libya. The Allied conquest of Vichy Madagascar in 1942 also was an unsettling factor in the French island colony.

Nevertheless no startling changes for most of Africa's peoples followed the peace settlements with Germany, Japan, and their allies. Only the former Italian colonies were affected directly. Ethiopia had been restored, after some British hesitation, to Haile Selassie's government in 1941. Great Power rivalry prevented Libya, Eritrea, and Somaliland from falling to any new colonial rulers. By its peace treaty in 1947 Italy renounced all rights to its former colonies. Since the major powers were unable to agree on their future the issue was decided in the United Nations. Libya gained independence in 1951, while Eritrea was federated to Ethiopia in 1952, and Somaliland was placed under Italy as a United Nations trust territory in 1950. The Somali Republic, a union of British and Italian Somaliland, gained its independence in 1960.

In other African dependencies the former mandated colonies of the defunct League of Nations became trust territories of the United Nations. The Union of South Africa, however, refused to acknowledge the authority of the United Nations in South West Africa, a move which the United Nations, despite a ruling in its favor by the World Court, has proved powerless to reverse. In the other trust territories, however, the new international organization was so constituted as to treat its dependencies in a manner far different from the League of Nations. Both of the major great powers of the postwar period, the United States and the Soviet Union, had, for their own different reasons, a hostility to the continuance of colonial rule in an Africa where neither had colonies. And the membership of the United Nations, with its representation of Asian, Latin American, and African nations, contained many lesser powers even more dedicated to the ending of European colonial empires. The new climate of opinion was represented particularly among the members of the organization directly concerned with the former mandates, the Trusteeship Council. The period of limited and comfortable debate over colonial territories between the holders of the mandates—the system of the League of Nations—was now replaced by an increasingly active intervention by the Trusteeship Council to ensure that the occupying powers were doing all that was possible to prepare their charges for independence.

Even more significant for Africa was the change in the world climate of opinion concerning the future of the overseas colonial empires. The European nations possessing subordinate territories were no longer important major powers. Colonial questions were of far less importance to them than their internal struggles to rebuild their war-shattered economic and social fabrics. Above all there was the example of the crumbling European domination of Asia. India was given independence as the two nations of India and Pakistan by the British Labor government in 1947. British rule was ended also in Ceylon and Burma, while many of the remaining Asian territories of other European nations similarly underwent dramatic changes in status. The United States participated in the changes by its long-delayed granting of independence to the Philippines in 1946. The British decisions were especially significant for Africa. Once these initial steps were taken in Asia, it was clearly only a matter of time before all of Britain's dependencies were treated similarly. An indication of the new British attitude was the Development and Welfare Act of 1945, a measure based upon a similar act of 1940 which had been inspired by conditions in the West Indian colonies. It was designed to supply financial resources for social and economic development from the budget of the metropolitan power. The act, for example, favored the organization of African trade unions, an important step in the rise of an effective nationalism. A successful general strike of 1945 in Nigeria demonstrated the consequent new strength of such organizations. The British may have considered that what they regarded as their backward African colonies would achieve independence only in the most distant future, but events were not to follow this comfortable pattern.

France had initiated more immediate steps to reorganize its colonial system. Félix Eboué (he died in 1944), who had become governor general of French Equatorial Africa, considered that a reform of the colonial relationship was essential. Influenced by his opinions, the French government organized at Brazzaville in January and February of 1944 a major conference of colonial administrators to plan for the future. The meeting's significance was signalled by the presence of General de Gaulle. The delegates recommended the strengthening of African traditional institutions, called for a more decentralized structure for their colonial empire, and planned reforms for ending forced labor and for stimulating economic and social development. There also was to be created an assembly to represent all the states of the French Empire. Independence for the colonies was rejected. A leading interpreter of the French colonial past aptly has described the results of the Brazzaville meeting as a "more genuine assimilation flexibly interpreted."[7] The

7. John D. Hargreaves, *West Africa: The Former French States* (Englewood Cliffs, N. J., 1967), p. 145.

future place of the empire was subsequently included in the deliberations of the Constituent Assembly of September 1945 which met to draw up the constitution for the new Fourth Republic. Over sixty colonial representatives were included in the membership of that assembly, including such African notables as the Senegalese politicians Léopold Senghor and Lamine Guèye. The first proposed constitution was defeated by French voters in April 1946, but a revised version was adopted in October. By the Fourth Republic's constitution, the colonies became overseas territories of an integral French Union; the French-run trust territories, because of their particular status, became associated members. All colonial subjects became French citizens, with the right of electing representatives to both the Fourth Republic's legislative body and a new consultative assembly of the French Union representing all of the components of the French world. The colonial representatives, however, were not given seats in the Chamber of Deputies in proportion to their populations: by the 1946 constitution the colonies were awarded twenty-three seats (by 1956 the number had risen to thirty-three). In addition each colony was given an elected territorial assembly possessing limited legislative powers. A related subsequent measure was the creation in 1946 of an Investment Fund for Economic and Social Development (FIDES), a step which allowed the colonies to end their economically unrewarding policy of depending upon their own budgets for the necessary funds for development.

All Africans, naturally, were not satisfied with the prospects for slow change embodied in the French conception of the colonial future, but nonetheless it did open a rational path for a continuing dialogue between Frenchman and African in most parts of the continent. The one great exception to this pattern, which had increasing influence in the evolution of French colonial policy, was the increasingly hostile relationship between the Muslim and French inhabitants of Algeria. During World War II most of the Muslim population of Algeria had remained loyal to their French rulers, their leaders hoping to gain postwar advances from this cooperation. Because of the French restrictions upon Messali al-Hajj and others the moderate Farhat Abbas emerged as the leading indigenous spokesman, emphasizing a policy calling for the future establishment of an Algerian state which somehow would be federated with France. His approach stimulated the hostility of both the French settlers and the more extreme followers of Messali. This first period ended when in May 1945 a disorganized rising against the government occurred. It was put down with excessive severity by the French.

The French solution to the unrest within Algeria was to place the North African territory within the new colonial system established after the conference at Brazzaville. Abbas and other Algerians participated in the Constituent Assembly of 1946 and subsequently were elected to the French legislature. In September 1947 the French government passed a special law establishing a new domestic Algerian system, giving that territory a precise political and economic status of its own, but within which the settlers secured a predominant influence. Algeria was given an assembly of two equal divisions possessing limited powers over the territorial budget. One division was elected by about 60,000 Frenchmen, the other by 1,300,000 Muslims. The concurrence of both was needed for action. And even this unequal distribution of power was made more unsatisfactory to the Muslims by the open rigging of the 1948 elections to the

Muslim division; the designation "Algerian elections" henceforth became in France a byword for dishonesty.

Without any legitimate outlet for their frustrations, some Muslim Algerians began to plan revolution. A Secret Organization was formed in 1948; its ranks included such participants as a future head of the independent Algerian state, Ahmad Ben Bella. The group began to use violence in 1949. The French, however, did not regard the movement as a serious threat to their rule until on November 1, 1954, in a series of seventy incidents of violence, the major Algerian revolution began. The revolutionary organization, calling itself the National Liberation Front, slowly gained a mass following as the French reacted violently, and with little discrimination as to actual involvement, against the Muslim population. By 1956 the settlers, with the support of the French army, were beyond the control of the increasingly weak governments of the Fourth Republic. Nevertheless they could not bring peace to an Algeria that was being devastated by the terrorist activities of the two conflicting parties.

Although by 1957 the settlers and the army considered that they were on the road to victory, the increasing international attention being focused on Algeria led them to fear that a political settlement by a war-weary French government and people might undercut their cause. In May 1958 the army allowed the settlers to rise against the French government, starting the events which returned de Gaulle to power in June. This determined French leader at first attempted to build a middle party in Algeria, between the European and Muslim extremes, by promising after the cessation of hostilities an eventual fair decision in the territory which could lead to an independent Algeria.

Neither contending side was satisfied with this policy. In January 1960 the settlers rose once more. This time, however, the army remained loyal to its government and the settlers were checked. Later, in April 1961, the French generals in Algeria did try to overthrow de Gaulle, but by this time most Frenchmen were no longer willing to endure continued war for the preservation of the rights of the settlers. Despite a harsh terroristic campaign by settler organizations, negotiations at last were entered into with the revolutionary government. They ended with the recognition of an independent Algeria in March 1962. Most of the settlers, fearing retaliation for their acts of terror, fled the country, leaving the exhausted Muslim Algerians to work out the future of their devastated homeland. The events of the Algerian revolution were a tragedy for both the Muslim and European inhabitants of the French territory. Fortunately, in the rest of French Africa, with the exception of the limited rising in Madagascar in 1947, the path to African independence followed a different evolution.

In the several colonies of French West Africa, for example, the changes of the 1946 constitution of the Fourth Republic had increased the electorate to about 1,000,000 individuals. Even though France still maintained dominant influence in many fields, including economic development, changes came rapidly. In the Ivory Coast economic progress allowed significant political development. Prosperity came to this coastal colony from the largely African cultivation of cotton and cocoa. To protect their position, the growers organized themselves under the leadership of a wealthy cultivator and Baoulé chief, who was also a doctor in the Assistance Médicale Indigène, Félix Houphouët-Boigny. He inevitably became involved in the unfolding political life of the postwar era, beginning with the Constituent Assembly of 1946. The eventual result was his leadership of the efficient Democratic Party of the Ivory Coast. Another course of African advance was the growth of trade unions, especially those of Guinée under the able leadership of Sékou Touré, which achieved an effective direction free of non-African influences. Other future African leaders emerged from the increased French commitment to education for Africans, much of which had to be carried on in France since there had been little development in West Africa. The young intellectuals, grouped from 1947 around the publication *Présence Africaine,* edited by Alioune Diop, with support from such notables as Léopold Senghor and Frantz Fanon, originally stressed African cultural autonomy as a reaction to French assimilationist policy. Later they turned to the closely related political problems of the day.

The postwar international scene, as discussed earlier, as well as the specific occurances within the French colonial world, had its influences in West Africa. The war from 1946 against the French in Indochina, with the searing defeat at Dien Bien Phu in 1954, cast a long shadow which was matched later by that of the Algerian holocaust. There was also a series of less traumatic events in Morocco, Tunisia, and Togo. In Tunisia, after World War I, nationalists had formed the Dastur Party; its goals included responsible government by a popularly elected assembly of Frenchmen and Tunisians. Little progress was made until a French-educated Tunisian, Habib Bourguiba, created the Neo-Dastur Party in 1934, a political group dedicated to gaining full independence for Tunisia. Progress was difficult, with little of note achieved by the outbreak of World War II. Thereafter Bourguiba maintained a steady pressure upon the French government, going beyond them in 1952 when all else failed, to appeal to the United Nations. The evolution of Moroccan politics then was also a subject of discussion in the United Nations. Modern Moroccan nationalism had developed at a slower pace, with little apparent impact being made before 1939. Nevertheless the Moroccan Sultan from 1927, Muhammad V, early began to oppose the French within the narrow limits open to him. The first effective nationalist group, the Istiqlal, was founded in 1943, even though many nationalist leaders had been jailed under wartime regulations. Nationalist agitation did not cease, however, continuing after the war with an increasing involvement by Muhammad V which led to his deposition and exile in 1951. When no progress resulted, either through peaceful internal means or through the United Nations, internal disorder occurred in both Tunisia and Morocco. The beginning of the Algerian revolution in 1954 led the French government to a more sympathetic attitude to their two protectorates. In 1956 a restored Muhammad V led Morocco to independence while Tunisia similarly achieved its independence under Bourguiba's leadership. Meanwhile in 1957 in British West Africa the Convention People's Party of Kwame Nkrumah had led the Gold Coast (renamed Ghana) to independence. The event had a direct influence in the neighboring French territory since the French felt it necessary to act to prevent a possible assimilation of French-administered Togo by an independent Ghana. The British-run portion of the Togo United Nations trust territory had agreed to join Ghana in 1956. Thus reforms were rapidly introduced to allow French Togo internal self-government. The Togo advance naturally served as a major stimulus to other French West African colonies.

African politicians had been working together to meet these many changes from 1946. In that year at Bamako they founded the Rassemblement Démocratique Africaine (RDA) to strive for African advances within the new French colonial system. The gaining of territorial independence was not an immediate goal. The leader of the RDA, Houphouët-Boigny, originally accepted an alliance with the French Communist Party, but by 1950, when he realized that the Communists were as committed to an assimilationist policy as other Frenchmen, the African organization stood on its own. During this period many other African leaders had cooperated with the French Socialists. They too began seeking their own path. Senghor, for example, founded the Bloc Démocratique Sénégalaise in 1948, reaching beyond the voters of the old four communes of Senegal to encompass the new rural voters of the hinterland.

Most of these African leaders looked originally to a continuation of the large French federation of West Africa, but the laws of 1946, which allowed assemblies only in individual territories, began a natural focusing of attention within each segment of the federation. A law of 1956 further increased this development by opening the way for additional local advances along the lines of the concessions given Togo. A particularly important defection from the ideal of unity was that of Houphouët-Boigny of the Ivory Coast, when doubts emerged within that prosperous colony about allowing the diversion of its resources into other, less favored neighboring states. The final break came under the Fifth French Republic. By this time, following the long wars in Indochina and Algeria, Frenchmen were no longer interested in any major struggles to retain colonies. The remaining dependencies of France were offered a choice between full internal self-government within a French Community (in which France would have a majority vote, plus control of foreign policy, defense, and economic affairs), and complete independence. De Gaulle clearly informed the colonial voters that a choice for the latter meant an immediate end to all French aid. Only in Guinée, where Sékou Touré's disciplined party gained 97 percent of the vote, did a colony opt for independence. Guinée's decision was met with an immediate, economically dislocating French withdrawal. This vindictive step has been well described as "one of the sorriest chapters in French post-war colonial administrations."[8] The other eight states of the federation, plus the remaining French territories in the rest of Africa, continued to work with France. But they were caught up in the rush of African states to full self-government: all except French Somaliland and the Comoro Islands achieved a peaceful independence in 1960. This independence was given with a good grace by de Gaulle's government, which wished to avoid any repeat of the earlier rupture with Guinée.

Many Africans continued to complain after 1960 of the large French role within the newly independent states. There were, for example, 30,000 Frenchmen residing in Dakar. Most of them, however, in Senegal and elsewhere, were engaged in administrative or business occupations, and were not permanent residents. Racial discrimination was rare, although differences in economic status led to racial segregation, while differences in educational levels hindered personal mingling. But this continuing French presence, which was modified in the years after independence, was the choice of African governments. It was open to future

8. L. Gray Cowan, "Guinea," in Gwendolen M. Carter, ed., *African One-Party States* (Ithaca, N. Y., 1962), p. 171.

evolution. French and African leaders had performed in a statesmanlike manner to bring independence peacefully to the many peoples of the former French African empire.

After World War II, the evolution of relations between the British and their African colonial subjects also included wide extremes of policy, although the British escaped a tragedy comparable to the Algerian experience. This was partly because they had already sacrificed African aspirations in the independent Union of South Africa and in the self-governing colony of Southern Rhodesia. Only the entrenched European minority of Kenya remained to pose a major settler problem. The most significant early African progress occurred in the small but prosperous colony of the Gold Coast. Possessing a vociferous and well-educated elite, here as elsewhere in Africa the result of a successful cash crop cultivation and of their own efforts to acquire a Western education, the Gold Coast had had African participation in the political development of the colony since the middle of the nineteenth century. There had been Africans serving in the legislative council since 1850, although they had exercised only a minor influence until the close of World War II. Nevertheless the Gold Coast proved ready for the opportunities brought by the postwar world. After World War I Africans had begun organizing into political groupings. In 1920, influenced by the self-determination themes of the preceding wartime period, the British West African National Congress, led by Casely Hayford of the Gold Coast, had worked for reforms within the colonial system and for closer union among British West Africans. The organization, however, remained a narrow elite, with most of its limited influence being exercised in the Gold Coast. After Hayford's death in 1930 the movement lost vitality. In 1947 J. B.

Danquah and others founded the United Gold Coast Convention (UGCC), an organization aiming to secure African independence as quickly as possible for the colony through constitutional procedures. Danquah was a former close associate of Hayford: both men had founded the Gold Coast Youth Conference in 1929 to work for African social and economic advancement. The UGCC, however, was dominated by an elite which lacked any broad base of support among the majority of the African population. To gain this needed support, Kwame Nkrumah, an American-educated African, was appointed party secretary. Nkrumah succeeded in broadening the base of political protest, but he became increasingly disenchanted with the leadership of the UGCC. Finally he broke with the UGCC to found a new group, the Convention People's Party, which was devoted to disruptive but nonviolent tactics for the securing of independence. In the elections of 1951 to the legislative council Nkrumah's party dominated the voting, winning thirty-four out of thirty-eight seats contested on a party basis. Included among the newly elected was Nkrumah, who was then serving a jail sentence for political activity. The British governor, Charles Arden-Clark, wisely recognizing the political realities of the victory, released Nkrumah so that he might form a new government. Thereafter the path to independence was irreversible, with Nkrumah responsibly leading the colony to internal self-government in 1954 and to freedom in 1957 as the state of Ghana.

Ghana had not been the first British African dependency to gain independence after World War II. The North African territory of the Anglo-Egyptian Sudan, like the Gold Coast untroubled by a white settler population, had been ruled under an Anglo-Egyptian condominium since 1899. Effective direction, however, had always remained in British hands. By 1946 the Sudan had been promised an eventual self-governing status. Following tensions resulting from Egyptian efforts to maintain a control over the country, the Sudan achieved self-government in 1952 and independence in 1956. But the Sudan's northern location and its Arab dominated government did not allow it to make an impact among British African states equal to the independence of Ghana.

In East Africa Tanganyika was the first British territory to achieve independence. Because of Tanganyika's previously discussed status as a League of Nations mandated territory, there was no large, power-seeking European settler community attempting to frustrate African political goals. But there also had been no significant African participation in the territory's political life. At the beginning of World War II no representatives of the African majority had served in Tanganyika's central political organs, no elections among Africans had been held, and local government, where Africans had some role, had become stagnant. In addition, Tanganyika was one of the poorest of Britain's African colonies.

Nonetheless, because of the presence of reasonable African and European leadership, political advance came rapidly. The first African representatives were appointed to the legislative council in 1945; by 1948 the council had four African members. However these Africans, drawn from the more conservative elements of society, were not to become Tanganyika's leaders. While new African representatives were emerging, a British governor, Edward Twining, from 1949 began to attempt constitutional reform. The governor believed in equal representation in the legislative council for the three recognized racial groupings of the territory,

Africans, Europeans, and Asians (individuals of Indian and Pakistani origins). The Africans, the overwhelming majority of the population, were prepared to accept the consequent minority positon for a temporary period, while the Asians and the Europeans eventually accepted a system which ensured that they would not dominate Tanganyikan politics. Also, there was agreement that all representatives to the legislative council would be elected by a common role of voters of all races, thus assuring the probable elimination of Europeans of racist mentality. In 1955 the new legislative council comprised sixty-one members, thirty of them selected—ten from each—by the three racial groups.

These advances were made in the presence of some pressure from two sources. Since 1930, many of the politically concerned Africans of Tanganyika had been gathered within the ranks of the Tanganyika African Association (TAA), an organization whose membership was drawn largely from Africans who had received some Western education and who were in government service. Before 1948 the TAA had been concerned mostly with social affairs and the condition of its member's employment, but from that date it gradually became involved with politics. This was an important evolution since the TAA was the only African organization with branches located throughout the entire territory. The other source of pressure for political advance in Tanganyika was the United Nations, acting through the Trusteeship Council. Although the British administration always formally discounted its efforts at pressure, the opinions of the United Nations agency obviously had an impact.

An important turning came in 1954 when the Trusteeship Council agreed to hear Julius Nyerere, the president of the TAA since 1954, and the man who by the force of his talented leadership was to lead Tanganyika to independence. Born in 1922, the son of a chief of the small Zanaki group, Nyerere received his early education in government schools. Then in 1943 he went to East Africa's only institution of higher learning, at Makerere in Uganda, to secure an education diploma. After teaching in Tanganyika, Nyerere became one of the first Tanganyikans to study abroad, receiving a Master of Arts degree from the University of Edinburgh in 1952. On his return to his country Nyerere again entered the teaching profession, but his background ensured that he would become a leading political figure. Nyerere realized that the TAA was not the best organization for African political advancement. In July 1954 he and the other concerned Africans founded the Tanganyikan African National Union (TANU), the first avowedly African political organization in Tanganyika. When Nyerere addressed the Trusteeship Council in 1954 the reasoned eloquence of his presentation, which stressed the fact that political progress was not evolving rapidly enough, and that further delays could lead the African majority to adopt extreme measures to achieve their goals, impressed his listeners. The occasion clearly signaled the emergence of a new African leader whose views had to be considered.

Despite the many difficulties inherent in organizing a political body in a country with such a poor communications system as Tanganyika possessed, TANU made steady progress. By 1955 TANU claimed 100,000 members. In the September 1958 elections, under a system whereby all voters had to cast ballots for one candidate of each racial group, TANU secured a notable victory. With the encouragement of a new British governor, Richard Turnbull, who considered that the best policy for Tanganyika's future was the support of Nyerere, further African triumphs followed. TANU became the dominant political party, achieving victories in all subsequent elections. In 1960 Tanganyika attained responsible government with Nyerere as chief minister, and in December 1961 Nyerere led Tanganyika to complete independence. (In 1964 Tanganyika joined with Zanzibar to form Tanzania.) It had been a remarkable progress for all of Tanganyika's inhabitants, with all races participating in the triumph. Nyerere's victory heralded the arrival on the African political scene of one of the continent's most influential and imaginative spokesmen.

Tanganyika's northern neighbor, Kenya, with its aggressive settler minority, had a far more troubled path to independence. By the beginning of World War II the settlers and the British colonial administrators directed a political system which effectively kept Africans in a subordinate status. The events of the war increased the unfavorable African position. Supposedly because of the fears of an Italian invasion from their Somali and Ethiopian colonies, the British imposed a ban on all African political activity and sent African leaders into detention. The Europeans, meantime, built upon their usefulness to the wartime government to further consolidate their already formidable local position. The settlers, for example, utilized their power to institute African labor regulations to supply workers for their private estates.

The Africans of Kenya were not tardy in challenging this predominance once the Allies moved to victory. In October of 1944 a political party, the Kenya African Union, was formed to head the drive for political advancement. In 1947 Jomo Kenyatta, who had returned to Kenya from Britain the previous year, became its president. One sign of African political gain was the appointment in 1944 of the first African to serve on the legislative council. Nevertheless the united front of European settlers and British officials was able to prevent any significant realization of African demands concerned with solving such problems as the poor economic position of the Africans, the increasing hardships of African urban life, or the growing shortage of land.

The resulting frustrations felt by many Africans led to an outbreak of serious proportions against the European rulers of Kenya and their African allies. The Mau Mau movement, which led to the declaration of a state of emergency within Kenya in 1952, at last made it clear to the colonial rulers in London that the system which they had allowed to evolve could not satisfy the legitimate aspirations of the majority of Kenya's inhabitants. Atrocities committed against Mau Mau detainees in the Hola prison camp in 1959 further strengthened this metropolitan opinion. The British government, therefore, began to move away from policies allowing European domination. New constitutions of 1954, 1957, and 1960 increased African participation in Kenyan political life, and despite European countermeasures to retain as much of their privileged position as possible, the turn in policy was definitive. At the Lancaster House Conference of 1960 the responsibility for the future evolution of Kenya passed to the Africans. Despite a split in African opinion concerning how the future independent Kenya should be organized, resulting in the formation of two political parties, the Kenya African National Union of Jomo Kenyatta and the Kenya African Democratic Party, the African advance continued. In December 1963 Kenya gained independence under the leadership of its veteran political figure, Jomo Kenyatta. Those Europeans who could not accept the new conditions of equal citizenship left the country, but many others remained to share in the building of the new African nation.

In the rest of Britain's African empire independence came to most colonies with relative ease during the 1960s. Nigeria attained independence in 1960, Sierra Leone in 1961, Uganda in 1962, Zambia (formerly Northern Rhodesia), Malawi (formerly Nyasaland), and Zanzibar in 1964, Gambia in 1965, Botswana (formerly Bechuanaland) and Lesotho (formerly Basutoland) in 1966, and Swaziland and Mauritius in 1968. The single discordant event in the process was the 1965 unilateral declaration of independence by the white-controlled government of Rhodesia (formerly Southern Rhodesia). The British government took no significant action to counter the Rhodesian decision.

Belgium, the remaining European colonial power with a parliamentary democracy at home, never evolved a reasoned policy leading its Congo territory to independence. The Belgians instead perceived this happening at so distant a date in the future that it could not be a serious policy objective. When a Belgian professor spoke in 1955 of independence for the Congo in thirty years, he was met with ridicule. Thus although the Belgian policy of social advancement for Africans was continued after World War II, with, for example, the founding of Lovanium University, no adequate measures were designed to prepare the African elites of the country for the complications of directing an independent African nation. Africans were not even allowed into the higher branches of the civil service until 1958, while acts of discrimination continued throughout the 1950s. African leaders, who were willing to work alongside Europeans, including the future major Congolese politician Patrice

Lumumba, consequently had little chance to do so. While following this inadequate policy the Belgian state became incapable of reacting effectively to a serious colonial crisis. The colonial block within Belgium declined in the 1950s, partly due to domestic political reasons, with the result that there was no possibility of the Belgians utilizing military means to retain their colony. In fact, a clause of the Belgian constitution forbade the use of draftees in the Congo. Thus when serious African riots occurred in the Congo's capital, Leopoldville, in January 1959, the Belgians were not disposed to contest seriously their colony's drive to independence. In 1960 when the Congolese political leaders momentarily achieved a united front, the decision was made for the creation of an independent Congo. The new state (which was renamed Zaire in 1971), with few personnel trained for the responsibilities thrust upon them, had to endure one of the most turbulent post independence periods in all of the continent. The colonies of Rwanda and Burundi, administered by Belgium as United Nations trust territories, gained their independence in 1962.

Portugal, the remaining important European colonial nation, chose not to participate in the decolonization process. The authoritarian government of Antonio de Oliveira Salazar, in power from 1926, affirmed that its African territories of Guinea, Moçambique, and Angola were integral parts of the Portuguese state. The policy has been continued by the government which followed the retirement of Salazar in 1968. However, most African subjects of Portugal remained untouched by that nation's limited efforts at assimilation. In 1950 only 2% of Angola's population was literate; the figure for Moçambique was 0.5%. The territories, respectively, then included 30,000 and 4,300

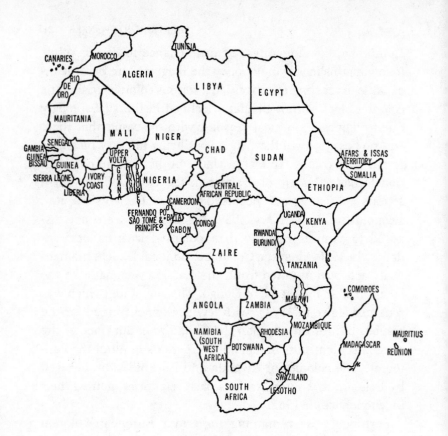

Africa Today

assimilated Africans. And post-World War II developments further increased the gap between the theories and the realities of Portuguese African policy. The boom in coffee production in Angola, for example, which made it the leading African exporter of that crop, as well as other economic advances, instead turned the Portuguese to inaugurate a policy of increased European settlement. From 1930 to 1960 the Portuguese population of Angola and Moçambique increased sixfold. There were 172,000 in Angola by 1960. The inevitable consequence was an increase in the number of Africans affected by forced-labor policies and the stressing of new economic policies which were devoted to the advancement of the European sector. Lacking other means of expressing their grievances, the Africans of all three colonies took up arms against their European rulers—in Angola in 1961, in Guinea in 1963, and in Moçambique in 1964. But by the early 1970s the Portuguese had managed to contain these continuing rebel movements, leaving to an uncertain future the fate of the territories of Africa's oldest continuing major European colonial empire.

6 Conclusion

The forms of contact between Europeans and Africans have changed in African territories following the successful attainment of independence by most of Europe's former colonies. The old relationship remains, however, in a few African countries. They include the Republic of South Africa (which left the British Commonwealth in 1961 because of criticism of its oppressive racial policies), Rhodesia, and the Portuguese colonies (plus a few minor French possessions). In most of them the future of the African majority remains unclear. The uncertain efforts of the divided United Nations, plus the military and economic weakness of the independent African states, ensure that the alien rule of Africans by European minorities will continue for some time to prevent the achievement of independence for all of Africa's indigenous inhabitants. Nevertheless the white-run states of southern Africa remain an unfortunate anachronism in the total African environment. The new nations of independent Africa will continue to develop, as Africans have throughout their history, by absorbing and reinterpreting the influences brought by Europeans, and now increasingly by Asians and Americans.

In the meantime there is considerable debate over the question of evaluating the impact of the years of European contact, and especially of the period of colonial rule, upon Africans. Most answers to this historical evaluation stem from the individual observer's reaction to the moral question arising out of the action of one people in imposing by force their rule upon another. The question is difficult to answer for many because of the problems involved in defining at what level an ethnic group "deserves" the right to self-determination. Postindependence strife in the African nations of the Congo, Nigeria, the Sudan, and Burundi, among others, demonstrates the complexity of the issue. But any rational judgment of the colonial era must be against the European conquest and rule of Africa. How many Frenchmen, for example, defend the conquest and occupation during World War II of their country by Germany? Nonetheless, other questions remain to be answered by the historian. The European conquerors certainly did have major influences with Africa which, for better or worse, modified, if not in absolute fashion at least in the pace of change, the course of the continent's evolution.

After the often bloody era of the European conquest, the general peace established by the new rulers, which was maintained through a continuous threat of force, did allow a security which accompanied the fundamental changes accomplished within the newly drawn boundaries of the colonial states. Such changes included the creation of monetary economies linked to the entire outside world, the establishment of territorywide modern transport systems, the introduction of Western medical techniques, and the development of a new urban class which replaced the older rural leadership as the seminal force within most African societies. Africans of course responded, as we have seen, in many varying ways to the changes brought or inspired by European rule. The old societies of Africa did not disappear completely, but rather they attempted to take what they thought best from their alien masters.

But it certainly must be remembered that many of the changes which did occur probably would have transpired, because of the pressure of European society on all nations in the world, even without the presence of imperial European intruders. Ethiopia, apart from its brief Italian occupation ending in 1941, managed to set itself upon the path of modernization without direct European rule. Both Egypt and Tunisia also began the process before they fell under the domination of Britain and France. And if the new ideas proceeded slowly in Ethiopia, they at least did occur without the intense psychological frustration that marked the relationships between Africans and Europeans in societies subservient to the dictates of masters possessing very different cultures. The Asian nations of Japan (before the American occupation following World War II) and Thailand are illustrative of parallel independent lines of development similar to those of Ethiopia.

Whatever the lingering scars of the past originating in the colonial relationship between Europeans and Africans, the ties between the two continents must continue in a world where distances are ever shrinking. For reasons of investment, national prestige, or simply because of the former ties forged between masters and subjects, the old relationships will persist in different ways. France, for example, in 1966 had about 6,000 of its nationals serving as teachers paid by the French government in various nations of Africa. The African states which gained independence have had little choice but to accept the boundaries left to them by Europeans, no matter what ethnic distortions remain. Within these boundaries the new nations are adapting the political patterns left by their former rulers to the traditions of their own developing societies. Whether this results in a continuation of the basic Western democratic processes of parliamentary government, the rule of military officers (often trained in Western countries) through the usurpation of power by forceful means, or the development of one-party states, the final determination of their usefulness must now be evaluated by the benefits, or lack thereof, which the new systems bring their citizens.

For the historian, the fact remains that the paths of Africa and Europe have been intertwined for thousands of years. Each continent has influenced the other by the mutual exchange of ideas and peoples. Moral judgments must be made upon this enduring relationship, but they should be based upon the increasing amount of accurate scholarship which is now becoming available to illuminate the many ties which have existed between Africans and Europeans all over the African continent.

Bibliographical Note

This bibliographical note contains only a selected list of works available in the English and French languages. For additional listings see the works of Murdock, Rotberg, and Hallett listed below. The various bibliographies issued by the International African Institute of London are very helpful. And, since African history is a rapidly changing field, the book review sections of the *Journal of African History*, *The International Journal of African Historical Studies*, and the *Journal of Modern African Studies* provide useful information on new sources.

For a general introduction to the African continent and its peoples Paul Bohannan and Philip Curtin, *Africa and Africans* (Garden City, N.Y., 1971), and John N. Paden and Edward W. Soja, eds., *The African Experience*, 3 vols. (Evanston, 1970-71), provide useful information. The geography of Africa can be studied in Dudley L. Stamp, *Africa: A Study in Tropical Development* (New York 1953, and succeeding editions), and Alan B. Mountjoy and Clifford Embleton, *Africa: A New Geographical Survey* (New York, 1967). For the many differing peoples of Africa, the reader may consult Simon and Phoebe Ottenberg, eds., *Cultures and Societies of Africa* (New York, 1960); James L. Gibbs, Jr., ed., *Peoples of Africa* (New York,

1960); and George P. Murdock, *Africa: Its Peoples and their Culture History* (New York, 1959). For the political systems of African peoples, see Meyer Fortes and E. E. Evans-Pritchard, eds., *African Political Systems* (London, 1940); John Middleton and David Tait, eds., *Tribes without Rulers* (London, 1958); and Ronald Cohen and John Middleton, *From Nation to Tribe in Africa* (San Francisco, 1970). The changing African social scene is well portrayed in P. C. Lloyd, *Africa in Social Change* (Baltimore, 1967).

J. Desmond Clark, *The Prehistory of Africa* (New York, 1970), offers the best synthesis of Africa's early history. Among the many general survey volumes on African history Robert I. Rotberg, *A Political History of Africa* (New York, 1965), and Robin Hallett, *Africa to 1875; A Modern History* (Ann Arbor, 1970), are useful volumes, while the somewhat dated *A Short History of Africa* (Baltimore, 1962) by Ronald Oliver and J. D. Fage remains of considerable value. J. D. Fage's *An Atlas of African History* (London, 1965) is an essential volume. A convenient collection of the more important articles on African history is Robert O. Collins, ed., *Problems in African History* (Englewood Cliffs, N. J., 1968). For the development of Islam in Africa, see P. M. Holt, Ann K. S. Lambton, and Bernard Lewis, eds., *The Cambridge History of Islam,* 2 vols. (Cambridge, 1970).

The early expansion of Europe can be followed in J. H. Parry, *The Age of Reconnaissance* (London, 1963). Philip D. Curtin's *The Atlantic Slave Trade: A Census* (Madison, 1969) provides the only reliable estimate of the magnitude of the African slave trade, while the same author's edited work, *Africa Remembered: Narratives by West Africans from the Era of the Slave Trade* (Madison, 1967), gives African accounts of that trade. Roger Anstey in his "A Reinterpretation of the Abolition of the British Slave Trade, 1806-1807," *The English*

Historical Review 87 (1972):304-32, offers the most convincing account of the beginning movement to end the slave trade. The development of European attitudes towards Africans, including the rise of racism, is detailed in Philip D. Curtin's stimulating *The Image of Africa* (Madison, 1965).

The exploration of Africa may be followed in Robin Hallett, *The Penetration of Africa* (London, 1965); Robert I. Rotberg, ed., *Africa and its Explorers: Motives, Methods, and Impact* (Cambridge, 1970); and in the introduction to *Stanley's Despatches to the New York Herald, 1871-1872, 1874-1877* (Boston, 1970), edited by Norman Robert Bennett.

An excellent beginning volume for the period of modern European colonization in Africa is D. K. Fieldhouse, *The Colonial Empires: A Comparative Survey from the Eighteenth Century* (New York, 1966). A briefer treatment for Africa alone is Robert O. Collins, *Europeans in Africa* (New York, 1971). For the partition of Africa, William Langer, *The Diplomacy of Imperialism* (New York, 1956), and Ronald Robinson, John Gallagher, and Alice Denny, *Africa and the Victorians: The Official Mind of Imperialism* (London, 1965), are major volumes. Several collections of readings offer a rich selection of the many authors offering explanations for the partition of Africa. They are Robert O. Collins, ed., *The Partition of Africa: Illusion or Necessity?* (New York, 1969); Ralph A. Austen, ed., *Modern Imperialism: Western Overseas Expansion and its Aftermath, 1776-1965* (Lexington Mass., 1969); Louis L. Snyder, ed., *The Imperialism Reader: Documents and Readings on Modern Expansionism* (Princeton, 1962); and Raymond F. Betts, ed., *The "Scramble for Africa": Causes and Dimensions of Empire* (Boston, 1966). There are useful collections of articles in *Colonialism in Africa, 1870-1960,* 3 vols. (Cambridge, 1969-71), the first two volumes of which were edited by L. H. Gann and Peter Duignan and the third by Victor Turner, and in the two volumes edited by Prosser Gifford and Wm. Roger Louis: *Britain and Germany in Africa: Imperial Rivalry and Colonial Rule* (New Haven, 1967), and *France and Britain in Africa: Imperial Rivalry and Colonial Rule* (New Haven, 1971). For the French colonial empire in Africa the following are recommended: Henri Blet, *Histoire de la Colonisation Française,* 3 vols. (Paris and Grenoble 1946-50); Henri Brunschwig, *French Colonialism, 1871-1914: Myths and Realities* (New York, 1964); J. Ganiage, *L'Expansion Coloniale et la France sous la Troisième République, 1871-1914* (Paris, 1968); and Raymond F. Betts, *Assimilation and Association in French Colonial Theory, 1890-1914* (New York, 1961). The important role of European missions in Africa is surveyed in C. P. Groves, *The Planting of Christianity in Africa,* 4 vols. (London, 1948-58). Another aspect of the colonial relationship is presented in *Africa and the West: Intellectual Responses to European Culture* (Madison, Wis., 1971), edited by Philip D. Curtin.

The massive collection of essays, *Power and Protest in Black Africa* edited by Robert I. Rotberg, and Ali A. Mazrui (New York, 1970), reaches from the colonial period up to the present. Other general volumes of interest relating to the period after World War II are John Hatch, *A History of Postwar Africa* (New York, 1965); Rupert Emerson and Martin Kilson, eds., *The Political Awakening of Africa* (Englewood Cliffs, 1965); Ndabaningi Sithole, *African Nationalism* (London, 1968); Gabriel A. Almond and James S. Coleman, *The Politics of Developing Areas* (Princeton, 1960); Gwendolen M. Carter, ed., *African One-Party States* (Ithaca, N. Y., 1962); and Gwendolen M. Carter, ed., *National Unity and Regionalism in Eight African States* (Ithaca, N. Y., 1966).

Many of the best works of African history are volumes dealing with the various regions of the continent. A selective listing follows.

Northern Africa

Abun-Nasr, Jamil M. *A History of the Maghrib* (Cambridge, 1971)

Bell, H. I. *Egypt from Alexander the Great to the Arab Invasion* (London, 1948)

Berque, Jacques. *French North Africa: The Maghrib between Two World Wars* (New York, 1962)

Brace, Richard M. *Morocco—Algeria—Tunisia* (Englewood Cliffs, N. J., 1964)

Collins, Robert O., and Tignor, Robert L. *Egypt and the Sudan* (Englewood Cliffs, N. J., 1967)

Courtois, C. *Les Vandales et l'Afrique* (Paris, 1955)

Diehl, C. *L'Afrique Byzantine* (Paris, 1896)

Gallagher, Charles F. *The United States and North Africa: Morocco, Algeria, and Tunisia* (Cambridge, 1963)

Hill, R. L. *Egypt in the Sudan, 1820-1881* (London, 1958)

Holt, P. M. *Egypt and the Fertile Crescent, 1516-1922* (London, 1966)

————*The Mahdist State in the Sudan, 1881-1898* (Oxford, 1958)

————*A Modern History of the Sudan* (London, 1961)

Juliene, Charles-André. *Histoire de l'Algérie Contemporaine: La Conquête et les Débuts de la Colonisation (1827-1871)* (Paris, 1964)

————*History of North Africa: From the Arab Conquest to 1830* (New York, 1970)

Picard, G. *Carthage* (London, 1964)

Sanderson, George N. *England, Europe, and the Upper Nile* (Edinburg, 1965)

Tignor, Robert L. *Modernization and British Colonial Rule in Egypt, 1882-1914* (Princeton, 1966)

Warmington, B. *Carthage* (Baltimore, 1960)

Western Africa

Ajayi, J. F. A. *Christian Missions in Nigeria, 1841-1941* (London, 1965)

——and Crowder, Michael, eds. *History of West Africa,* vol. 1 (New York, 1972)

Coleman, James S. *Nigeria: Background to Nationalism* (Berkeley and Los Angeles, 1958)

Crowder, Michael. *Senegal: A Study of French Assimilation Policy* (London, 1967)

——*West Africa under Colonial Rule* (Evanston, Ill., 1968)

——and Ikime, Obaro, eds., *West African Chiefs: Their Changing Status under Colonial Rule and Independence* (New York, 1970)

Fage, J. D. *A History of West Africa: An Introductory Survey* (Cambridge, 1969)

Flint, John E. *Nigeria and Ghana* (Englewood Cliffs, N. J., 1966)

Fyfe, Christopher. *A History of Sierra Leone* (Oxford, 1962)

Hargreaves, John D. *Prelude to the Partition of West Africa* (New York, 1966)

——*West Africa: The Former French States* (Englewood Cliffs, N. J., 1967)

Johnson G. Wesley, Jr. *The Emergence of Black Politics in Senegal: The Struggle for Power in the Four Communes, 1900-1920* (Stanford, 1971)

Kanya-Forstner, A. S. *The Conquest of the Western Sudan: A Study in French Military Imperialism* (Cambridge, 1969)

Kimball, David. *A Political History of Ghana: The Rise of Gold Coast Nationalism, 1850-1928* (Oxford, 1963)

Liebenow, J. Gus. *Liberia: The Evolution of Privilege* (Ithaca, N. Y., 1969)

Lynch, Hollis R. *Edward Wilmot Blyden: Pan-Negro Patriot, 1832-1912* (New York, 1967)

Priestley, Margaret. *West African Trade and Coast Society: A Family Study* (London, 1969)

Webster, J. B., Boahen, A. A., and Idowu, H. O. *History of West Africa: The Revolutionary Years—1815 to Independence* (New York, 1970)

Weinstein, Brian. *Eboué* (New York, 1972)

Eastern Africa

Apter, David E. *The Political Kingdom in Uganda: A Study in Bureaucratic Nationalism* (Princeton, 1967)

Bennett, Norman Robert, ed. *Leadership in Eastern Africa: Six Political Biographies* (Boston, 1968)

Bennett, Norman Robert. *Mirambo of Tanzania, ca. 1840-1884* (New york, 1971)

Chidzero, B. T. G. *Tanganyika under International Trusteeship* (London, 1961)

Deschamps, Hubert. *Histoire de Madagascar* (Paris, 1961)

Fallers, L. A., ed. *The King's Men: Leadership and Status in Buganda on the Eve of Independence* (London, 1964)

Gwassa, G. C. K., and Iliffe, John, eds. *Records of the Maji Maji Rising,* Historical Association of Tanzania Paper No. 4 (Nairobi, 1967)

Harlow, Vincent, Chilver, E. M., and Smith, Alison. *History of East Africa,* vol. 2 (Oxford, 1965)

Hess, Robert L. *Ethiopia: The Modernization of Autocracy* (Ithaca, N.Y., 1970)

———*Italian Colonialism in Somalia* (Chicago, 1966)

Hesseltine, Nigel. *Madagascar* (New York, 1971)

Iliffe, John. *Tanganyika under German Rule, 1905-1912* (Cambridge, 1969)

Kenyatta, Jomo. *Facing Mount Kenya* (New York, n.d.)

Kimambo, I. N., and Temu, A. J., eds. *A History of Tanzania* (Nairobi, 1969)

Kent, Raymond. *Early Kingdoms in Madagascar, 1500-1700* (New York, 1970)

Lewis, I. M. *The Modern History of Somaliland* (London, 1965)

Mangat, J. S. *A History of the Asians in East Africa, c. 1886 to 1945* (Oxford, 1969)

Ogot, B. A., and Kieran, J. A., eds., *Zamani: A Survey of East African History* (New York, 1968)

Oliver, Roland, *The Missionary Factor in East Africa* (London, 1952)

――――and Mathew, Gervase, eds., *History of East Africa*, vol. 1 (Oxford, 1963)

Rosberg, Carl G., and Nottingham, J. *The Myth of "Mau Mau": Nationalism in Kenya* (Nairobi, 1967)

Rowe, John A. *Lugard at Kampala*, Makerere History Paper No. 3 (Kampala, 1969)

Wolff, Richard D. *The Economics of Colonialism: Britain and Kenya, 1870-1930* (New Haven, 1974)

Central and Southern Africa

Anstey, Roger. *King Leopold's Legacy: The Congo under Belgian Rule* (Oxford, 1966)

Axelson, E. *The Portuguese in South-East Africa, 1600-1700* (Johannesburg, 1960)

――――*South-East Africa, 1488-1530* (London, 1940)

Birmingham, D. *Trade and Conflict in Angola: The Mbundu and their Neighbours under the Influence of the Portuguese, 1483-1790* (Oxford, 1966)

Boxer, C. R. *Race Relations in the Portuguese Colonial Empire, 1415-1825* (Oxford, 1963)

Ceulemans, P. *La Question Arabe et le Congo (1883-1892)* (Brussels, 1959)

Chilcote, Ronald H. *Portuguese Africa* (Englewood Cliffs, N. J., 1967)

De Kiewiet, C. W. *A History of South Africa: Social & Economic* (London, 1941)

Denoon, Donald et al. *Southern Africa since 1800* (New York, 1972)

Duffy, James *Portuguese Africa* (Baltimore, 1963)
———*A Question of Slavery* (Cambridge, 1967)

Fagan, B. M. *Southern Africa during the Iron Age* (London, 1965)

Gann, Lewis H. *Central Africa: The Former British States* (Englewood Cliffs, N. J., 1971)

Hammond, R. J. *Portugal and Africa, 1815-1910: A Study in Uneconomic Imperialism* (Stanford, 1966)

Isaacman, Allen F. *Mozambique: The Africanization of a European Institution: The Zambezi Prazos* (Madison, Wis., 1972)

Langworthy, H. W. *Zambia before 1890: Aspects of Pre-Colonial History* (London, 1972)

Mason, Philip. *The Birth of a Dilemma: The Conquest and Settlement of Rhodesia* (London, 1958)

Newitt, M. D. D. *Portuguese Settlement on the Zambesi: Exploration, Land Tenure and Colonial Rule in East Africa* (New York, 1973)

Ranger, T. O., ed., *Aspects of Central African History* (Evanston, Ill., 1968)

Ranger, T. O. *Revolt in Southern Rhodesia, 1896-97* (Evanston, Ill., 1967)

Shepperson, George, and Price, Thomas. *Independent African: John Chilembwe and the Origins, Setting and Significance of the Nyasaland Native Rising of 1915* (Edingburgh, 1958)

Slade, R. *King Leopold's Congo* (London, 1962)

Stokes, Eric, and Brown, Richard, eds. *The Zambesian Past: Studies in Central African History* (Manchester, 1966)

Thompson, Leonard *The Unification of South Africa, 1902-1910* (Oxford, 1960)

Wheeler, Douglas L., and Pélissier, René. *Angola* (New York, 1971)

Wilson, Monica, and Thompson, Leonard, eds. *The Oxford History of South Africa,* 2 vols. (Oxford, 1969-70)

Index

Abbas, Farhat, 194-95, 202
Abd al-Aziz, Mawlay, 103
Abd al-Hamid ibn Badis, 195
Abd al-Qadir, 70-2, 103
Abd al-Rahman, Mawlay, 72
Abd Allahi ibn Muhammad, 109-10
Abduh, Muhammad, 185
Abukir Bay, 62
Adal, 39
Aduwa, 102
Affonso I (Mbemba Nzinga), 32-3
Afghani, Jamal al-Din al-, 185
Afikpo Ibo, 14
African Association, 76
Afrikaners, 64-5, 73, 163-64, 185
Afro-Americans, 105
Ahmad bin Husayn, 37-8
Ahmad ibn Ibrahim al-Ghazi (Ahmad Gran), 39-40
Ahmad bin Shaykh (Ahmadu Seku), 134
Akan, 30
Akwamu, 46
Alawite dynasty, 103
Albert, Lake, 80
Alexander the Great, 22
Alexandria, 187

Algeria, 63, 66, 68-75, 87, 95, 103, 125, 127-31, 133, 142, 150n, 151n, 194-96, 198, 202-07, 209
Algiers, 68-71, 74
Almeida, Francisco da, 51
Almeida e Albuquerque, Alexandre, 99
Almohads, see Muwahhidun, al-
Almoravids, see Murabitun, al-
Alsace, 92, 130
American Board of Commissioners to Foreign Missions, 177
American Colonization Society, 104
American Revolution, 53, 59
Americans, 27, 60, 81, 83, 106, 136, 197, 223
Americo-Liberians, 106
Amis des Noirs, Société des, 56
Anglo-Egyptian Sudan, 125, 143, 159, 187, 210
Ango, Jean, 43
Angola, 31, 34-5, 41-2, 45, 51, 75, 80, 99, 100, 161-62, 217, 219
Anthropological Society of Paris, 133

Arabi, Ahmad, 187
Archinard, Louis, 133
Arden-Clark, Charles, 210
Aruj, 68
Ashanti, 49, 98-9
Ashmun, Jehudi, 105
Assab, 101
Assyrians, 5
Atlantic Charter, 197
Augustine, 23
Augustus, 21
Axum, 6, 39

Badagri, 77
Baikie, W. B., 78
Baker, Samuel, 80, 109
Bamako, 207
Bangweulu, Lake, 82
Baoulé, 204
Baptist Missionary Society, 176
Baratieri, Oreste, 102
Baring, Evelyn (Lord Cromer), 110
Barotseland, 157
Barruoua, 97
Barth, Heinrich, 83
Basuto, Basutoland, 65, 143, 216
Bechuanaland, 143, 216
Beira, 36
Belgium, 84, 88-9, 107-08, 125, 147, 159-61, 180, 184, 216-17
Bella, Ahmad Ben, 203
Benin, 13, 33-4, 111
Bennett, James G., 81
Benue, River, 6
Berbers, 18, 21

Berlin Act, 93, 160
Berlin Conference, 92-3, 96
Bismarck, Otto von, 91-2, 96, 130
Bloc Démocratique Sénégalaise, 207(a)
Bloemfontein Convention, 65
Blum, Leon, 142
Blum-Violette Bill, 196
Boer War, 85, 153, 185
Bokero cult, 169
Boma, 90
Bond of 1844, 98
Borgu, 97
Bornu, 17
Botswana, 216
Bourbon, see Réunion
Bourguiba, Habib, 205-06
Brandenburg, 46
Brazil, 30, 44-5, 60
Brazza, Pierre Savorgnan de, 89-90
Brazzaville, 200, 202
Briere de l'Isle, Gaston, 133
Bristol, 45
Britain, British, 34, 42, 45-6, 48, 56-7, 59-61, 63-5, 73-6, 80-5, 87-93, 95-111, 113-17, 125, 127, 132, 135-36, 139, 141, 143-48, 150-52, 154-56, 158-60, 163-65, 171, 173-75, 177, 180, 187, 192-93, 197-200, 209-12, 214-16, 221, 223
British East India Co., 43
British National African Co., 92, 97
British South Africa Co., 172-74

British West Africa National Congress, 209
Bruce, James, 54, 78
Brué, André, 44, 66
Bruxelles Conference (1876), 89
Buganda, 10-2, 15, 79, 97, 114-16, 135, 143, 148-51
Bugeaud, Thomas Robert, 71-3, 131
Bunyoro, 10-1, 117
Burton, Richard F., 79
Burundi, 16, 108, 147, 161, 217, 222
Bushmen, *see* San
Byzantines, 24

Cairo, 17
Cambon, Paul, 95
Cameron, Donald, 146, 148
Cameron, Verney L., 83
Cameroun, Cameroons, 125, 143
Cão, Diogo, 29, 31
Cape Coast, 45
Cape Colony, 74, 164-65
Cape Colored peoples, 52
Cape Town, 51, 53, 64
Caracalla, 22
Carthage, 17, 19, 20-2, 24
Casement, Roger, 160
Ceuta, 28
Chad, 125, 196
Chad, Lake, 97, 125
Chagga, 15, 113-14, 168
Chamberlain, Joseph, 97
Charles X, 68-9
China, 30

Christianborg, 46
Churchill, Winston, 197
Church Missionary Society, 78, 176-78, 181
Church of Scotland, 192
Clapperton, Hugh, 77
Clarkson, Thomas, 56
Colbert, Jean Baptiste, 43
Committee of Merchants, 98
Comoro Islands, 75, 125, 208
Company of Merchants Trading to Africa, 45, 98
Company of Royal Adventurers Trading to Africa, 45
Congo, *see* Zaire
Congo Independent State, 93, 117-20, 159-61, 184, 216-17, 222
Congo Reform Association, 160
Congo River, 4, 31, 41, 78, 82-3, 89-93, 117
Consolidated Goldfields of South Africa, Ltd., 164
Constantine, 70, 74
Convention People's Party, 206, 210
Crowther, Samuel, 177, 179
Curtin, Philip D., 49

Dahomey, 12, 49, 61-2, 97, 125-26
Daily Telepgraph, 82
Dakar, 125, 133, 141, 181, 208
Danakil, 39
Danquah, J.B., 209-10
Dar es Salaam, 171
Dastur Party, 205

Daudi Chwa, 149
David, Pierre Félix, 66
Deane, Walter, 118
De Beers Consolidated Mines, Ltd., 163
Decken, C. C. von, 83
De Gaulle, Charles, 196-97, 200, 203, 208
Delamere, Lord, 153
Denham, Dixon, 77
Denmark, Danes, 46, 54, 59
Dernburg, Bernard von, 170
Déval, Pierre, 68
Development and Welfare Act (1945), 199
Devonshire White Paper, 156
Dhanis, Francis, 119
Diagne, Blaise, 141, 190-91
Dias, Bartholomeu, 29
Dias de Novaes, Paulo, 34
Diop, Alioune, 205
Disraeli, Benjamin, 186
Dominican Order, 26
Donatists, 23
Durham University, 181
Dutch, 31, 41-2, 44-6, 50-4, 60, 64, 73, 75, 99, 185
Dutch East India Co., 43, 45, 51, 53
Dutch West India Co., 45

Eannes, Gil, 29
Eboué, Félix, 196-97, 200
Ecole Normale William Ponty, 181
Edinburgh, University of, 213

Egypt, Egyptian, 3-4, 21-2, 26, 62-3, 70, 78, 87-8, 104, 109-10, 117-18, 143, 185-88, 190, 211, 223
Elgin, Lord, 154
Eliot, Charles, 153-54
Emin Pasha, 118
Erhardt, Jacob, 78-9, 178
Eritrea, 102-03, 198
Ethiopia, 3n, 17, 39-40, 54, 78, 81, 101-04, 108, 110, 165, 197-98, 214, 223
Ezana, 39

Faidherbe, Louis, 67, 131-32
Fanon, Frantz, 205
Fanti, 49, 98-9
Fanti Confederation, 99
Farid, Muhammad, 187
Fashoda, 95, 100-01
Ferry, Jules, 95, 188
Fiftieth Ordinance (1828), 64
Firestone Rubber Co., 106
Fon, 49
Fort Jesus, 37-8
Fourah Bay College, 177, 181
France, French, 24, 42-3, 48, 54, 56, 60, 62-4, 66-75, 84, 87-93, 95-7, 100-04, 106, 108, 110, 114, 116, 119, 125-44, 150, 159, 177, 180-81, 186, 188-91, 194-98, 200-09, 221-24
Francis I, 42-3
Franciscan Order, 26
Free Town, 57, 75

French Equatorial Africa, 125, 196, 200
French Revolution, 53, 63, 68
French West Africa, 197, 204, 206
French West Indies Co., 43-4
Fulani, 18
Futa Jallon, 76

Gabon, 75, 89, 125
Galawdewos, 40
Gallieni, Joseph, 134-37
Gama, Christovão da, 40
Gama, Vasco da, 29
Gambia, 74, 76, 143
Ganda, 12, 14, 115-17, 148-49
Gandhi, Mahatma, 165
Garrison, William Lloyd, 105
German East Africa, 96, 106-08, 168-69, 174, 181
Germany, Germans, 73, 78, 84, 91-3, 95-7, 106-08, 110-15, 118, 120, 129-30, 146-47, 151, 158, 169-72, 182, 193, 198, 222
Ghana, 7, 206, 210-11
Girouard, Percy, 157
Gladstone, William, 96
Glele, 61
Gold Coast, 30, 44-7, 49, 74-5, 98-9, 143, 177, 183, 206, 209-10
Goldie, George, 92, 97
Gomes, Fernão, 29
Gordon, Charles, 109
Gorée, 67, 132-33

Grant, John A., 79-80
Great Trek, 64
Greeks, 1, 27
Guèye, Lamine, 201
Guinea, 41, 76, 100, 125, 161-62, 217, 219
Guinée, 184, 205, 208

Haile Selassie, 102, 198
Haiti, see Saint Domingue
Hannibal, 21
Hausa, 16, 77, 144
Haya, 147
Hayford, Casely, 209-10
Hehe, 111-12, 147, 168
Henry of Portugal, 28, 43
Herodotus, 78
Hippo, 23
Hola prison camp, 215
Holy Ghost Fathers, 178
Hottentot, see Khoikhoi
Houphouët-Boigny, Félix, 204, 207
Huguenots, 52
Huron, 126
Hussayn, Dey, 68-9

Ibo, 13-4, 143
Ile de France, see Mauritius
Imperial British East African Co., 115-16, 151-52
India, 30, 37, 127, 155, 158, 164, 199
Indian Congress Party, 190
Indochina, 133-34, 205
International African Association, 88-9

International Associaton of the Congo, 89

Investment for Economic and Social Development (FIDES), 201

Ismail, 109, 186

Istiqlal, 206

Italy, Italians, 84, 95, 101-04, 110, 197-98, 214, 223

Itsekiri, 34

Ivory Coast, 125, 150n, 204-05, 207

Jameson, Leander, 164, 173-74

Japan, 30, 198, 223

João I, *see* Nzinga Kuwu

Johnston, Harry, 148

Jones, William, 178

Juba River, 102

Justinian, 24

Kabarega, 117

Kagubi, 174

Kagwa, Apolo, 116

Kamerun, 92, 106, 108

Kamil, Mustafa, 187

Kano, 16, 77

Karari, 110

Kassar Said, treaty of, 95

Kenya, 78, 114, 143, 150-58, 172, 181, 191-94, 209, 214-15

Kenya African Democractic Party, 215

Kenya African National Union, 215

Kenya African Union, 214

Kenyatta, Jomo, 192-93, 214-15

Khartoum, 109-10

Khayr al-Din, 68

Khoikhoi, 7, 50-2, 64

Kiboshi, 113-14

Kigoma, 171

Kikuyu, 143, 153, 181, 191-93

Kikuyu Central Association, 192

Kikuyu Independent Schools Association, 182

Kilimanjaro, Mount, 15, 78, 113-14

Kilwa, 10, 16, 36, 169

Kimbangu, Simon, 184

Kirk, John, 96

Kisumu, 152

Kitawala, 184

Kitchener, Herbert, 100-01, 109-10

Kolelo cult, 169

Kongo kingdom, 31, 33-4, 41, 90

Krapf, Johan, 78, 178

Kruger, Paul, 164

Kumbi-Salah, 7

Lagos, 60, 65, 97

Laird, Macgregor, 68

La Marsa, treaty of, 95

Lander, John, 67

Lander, Richard, 77, 84

Lausanne, treaty of, 104

Lavigérie, Cardinal, 120

League of Nations, 102, 108 158, 161, 190, 198, 211

Lebna Dengel, 39

Leclerc, Jacques, 197

Lenin, V. I., 85-6

Leopold II, 84, 88-93, 117-20, 159-60
Leopoldville, 217
Lesotho, 216
Lesseps, Ferdinand de, 186
Lettow-Vorbeck, Paul von, 107
Liberia, 104-06, 108, 177
Liberia, University of, 179
Libreville, 75
Libya, 103-04, 197-98
Lisbon, 33, 35, 41
Liverpool, 45, 78
Livingstone, David, 80-4, 118
Lobengula, 172
London, 45, 82, 98
London Missionary Society, 80, 176
London School of Economics, 193
Lorraine, 92, 130
Louis IX, 26
Louis Phillippe, 69, 128
Lovanium University, 216
Lozi, 143
Luanda, 34
Lüderitz, Adolf, 91
Lugalo, 112
Lugard, Frederick D., 97, 115-16, 144-45, 151, 156
Lugbara, 13, 143
Lukuga River, 83
Lumumba, Patrice, 216-17
Lunda, 17
Lwoo, 10
Lyautey, Louis, 137-39, 145

Mabanza, 31

Macarthy, Charles, 98
Mackinnon, William, 151
Maclean, George, 98
Madagascar, 51, 75, 125, 135-37, 139, 142-43, 150-51n, 198, 204
Mahdi, 100, 108-10, 118
Maji Maji rebellion, 168-71, 173-74
Makerere, 181, 213
Malawi, 97, 216
Malawi, Lake, 79, 81
Mali, 7
Malindi, 30
Malinowski, Bronislaw, 193
Mandara, 113
Mankessim, 99
Mansfield, Lord, 57
Marangu, 114
Marchand, Jean-Baptiste, 101
Marealle, 114
Marinids, 26
Maroons, 56
Marseille, 133
Marx, Karl, 85
Masai, 15, 153
Massawa, 102
Massinissa, 21
Matumbi, 169
Mau Mau, 214
Mauritius, 126, 143, 216
Mavura Mhande, 36-7
Mayotte, 95
Mbemba Nzinga, see Affonso I
Meli, 114
Menilik II, 101-02
Merina, 135-37, 139

Meroe, 5
Messali al-Hajj, 195, 202
Middle Congo, 125
Milner, Lord, 164
Mirambo, 120
Mitchell, Philip, 144
Mkwawa, 111-13, 147
Moçambique, 10, 37-8, 41-2, 75, 80, 99-100, 107, 161-62, 217, 219
Mogador, 72
Mombasa, 30, 35, 37-8, 152
Monomotapa, see Mwene Mutapa
Monroe, James, 104
Monrovia, 105
Montesquieu, Baron, 56
Morel, E. D., 160
Morocco, 25-6, 28, 41n, 72, 103-04, 125, 138, 145, 198, 205-06
Moshi, 113-14
Mpandashalo, 120
Muhammad V, 206
Muhammad Ahmad inn Abd Allah, 100, 108-09
Muhammad Ali, 63, 70, 109, 186
Munyigumba, 111
Murabitun, al-, 26
Mussolino, Benito, 102
Mutesa I, 11, 79, 83, 114-15
Muwahhidun, al-, 26
Mwanga, 115-16
Mwene Mutapa, 36

Nairobi, 153, 192

Napoleon I, 60, 62
Napoleon III, 74, 128-30
Natal, 65, 144, 164
National Liberation Front (Algeria), 203
Ndebele, 172-75
Ndongo, 34
Nehanda, 174
Nelson, Horatio, 62
Neo-Dastur Party, 205
New York Herald, 181-2
Ngola, 34
Ngongo Lutete, 119
Ngoni, 169
Niger, 125
Niger Convention, 98
Niger River, 4, 6, 49, 61, 75-9, 83, 92-3, 97, 132-33
Nigeria, 6, 13, 16, 76-7, 97-8, 111, 143-47, 157, 177, 180, 184, 200, 216, 222
Nile River, 3-4, 78-83, 100-01, 110
Nkrumah, Kwame, 206, 210
Nok, 6
Normans, 26
North African Star, 195
Northern Rhodesia, 107, 143, 157, 159, 216
Nosy Bé, 75
Nova Scotia, 57
Numidia, 23
Nyambo Kapararidze, 37
Nyamwezi, 79, 120, 168, 171
Nyangwe, 83
Nyasaland, 143, 216
Nyerere, Julius, 184, 212, 214

Nazinga Kuwu, 31-2

Ogowe River, 80
Omani Arabs, 38
Omdurman, 110
Oran, 70, 74
Orange Free State, 65, 163-65
Orange River, 50, 65
Ottoman Turks, 62-3, 68-9, 95, 104
Oubangui-Chari, 125, 159
Oudney, Walter, 77
Ouverture, Toussaint 1', 127

Paez, Pedro, 78
Pakistan, 199
Paris, 98, 128, 190
Paris Evangelical Society, 177
Paris Geographical Society, 133
Park, Mungo, 54, 76-7, 84
Pétain, Philippe, 196
Peters, Carl, 96
Phillippines, 199
Phoenecians, 6, 20
Portugal, Portuguese, 27-42, 44-8, 51, 60, 62, 75, 78, 84, 90-1, 100, 125, 161-63, 177, 217, 219, 221
Prester John, 29, 39-40
Ptolemy, 22, 78
Punic Wars, 21

Quaque, Philip, 47

Radama I, 135
Ranavalona I, 135-36

Rassemblement Démocratique Africaine, 207
Rebmann, Johann, 78, 178
Rechenberg, Albrecht von, 170-71
Réunion, 125
Revolution of 1848, 128
Rhodes, Cecil, 163-64, 172, 174-75
Rhodesia, 36, 216, 221
Richelieu, Cardinal, 43
Riebeeck, Jan van, 51
Rindi, 113-14
Roberts, Joseph, 105
Roger, Baron, 66
Romans, 1, 17, 19-25, 27, 30, 73
Roosevelt, Franklin D., 197
Rosetta Stone, 62
Royal Africa Co., 45
Royal Geographical Society, 79, 81
Royal Niger Co., 97
Rufisque, 133
Russian Revolution, 85
Ruvuma River, 81
Rwanda, 16, 108, 147, 161, 217

Sa'dian dynasty, 28
Sadiqi College, 188
Said of Egypt, 186
Saint Domingue, 56, 58, 126
Saint Louis (Senegal), 43-4, 67, 132-33
Salah al-Din (Saladin), 26
Salazar, Antonio de Oliveira, 217
San, 7, 52

Sand River Convention, 65
Sanusi brotherhood, 104
São Jorge da Mina, 39
São Salvador, 31
São Tomé, 33
Schmaltz, Julien, 66
Scotland, 80
Sebastian of Portugal, 41n
Sefu bin Muhammad, 119
Segu, 76
Senegal, 43-4, 53, 61, 66-7, 74-5, 125-26, 131-34, 141, 150n, 151n, 177, 184, 190, 201, 207, 208
Senegal Co., 44
Senegal River, 43
Senghor, Léopold Sédar, 184, 201, 205, 207
Septimus Severus, 22-3
Sharp, Granville, 56-7
Shepstone, Theophilus, 144
Shona, 172-75
Sierra Leone, 29, 56-7, 59, 74, 98-9, 105, 143, 177, 181, 216
Sierra Leone Co., 56-7
Silveira, Gonçalo de, 36
Sina, 113-14
Society for the Propagation of the Gospel, 47
Sofala, 36
Sokoto, 77, 145
Somaliland, 15, 39, 125-26, 143, 153, 192, 198, 208, 214
Somerset, James, 57
Songhai, 7
South Africa, 69, 73-5, 85, 87, 91, 107, 163

South Africa, Republic of, 221
Southern Rhodesia, 143, 150-51, 156-57, 172, 174, 209, 216
South West Africa, 91, 106, 108, 198
Soviet Union, 193, 198
Spain, Spaniards, 20-1, 26, 42, 54, 60, 74, 103-04, 126
Speke, John H., 79, 80, 83, 114
Stanley, Henry M., 27, 81-4, 89-90, 114, 118-20
Stanley Falls, 118-19
Strong, Josiah, 56
Sudan, 3n, 5, 7, 11, 25, 54, 100, 108-11, 117-18, 143, 211-22
Suez Canal, 87, 100, 186-87
Sukuma, 171, 183
Swahili, 10, 169
Swaziland, 143, 216
Sweden, Swedes, 46, 59
Switzerland, 85

Tabora, 79, 171
Tafna, 70
Tal al-Kabir, al-, 187
Tana River, 7
Tanga, 181, 183
Tanganyika, see Tanzania
Tanganyika African Association, 212-13
Tanganyika African National Union (TANU), 213-14
Tanganyika, Lake, 79, 82-3, 89, 119, 159, 171
Tangier, 72
Tanzania, 79-80, 96, 111, 120, 143, 146-48, 157-58, 166,

Tanzania, (cont.)
170, 181, 183-84, 211-14
Tawfiq, 186-87
Temne, 57
Tewodorus, 81
Thailand, 223
Theal, Geroge M., 48
Thuku, Harry, 191-92
Timbuktu, 76-7
Tippu Tip, 118-19
Togo, 92, 106, 108, 125, 143, 205-07
Tokolor, 132
Tongking, 134, 137
Tordesillas, treaty of, 42
Touré, Sékou, 184, 205, 208
Transvaal, 65, 163-65, 173
Tripoli, 77
Trusteeship Council of the U.N., 199, 212-13
Tunis, 20
Tunisia, 26, 95, 104, 125, 187-89, 198, 205-06, 223
Turnbull, Richard, 213
Tushki, 109
Tutsi, 16
Twining, Edward, 211

Uganda, 13, 116-17, 143-44, 148-49, 152, 181, 216
Ughoto, 34
Ujiji, 82
Umar, al-Hajj, 132, 134
Union of South Africa, 106, 108, 143, 153, 165, 175, 198, 209
United Gold Coast Convention, 210

United Nations, 197-98, 206, 212, 217, 221
United Native African Church, 184
United States of America, 59, 92, 105, 198-99
Universities' Mission to Central Africa, 178, 179
Unyanyembe, 79
Upper Volta, 125
Urambo, 120
Uthman dan Fodio, 144

Valentin, Durand, 67
Vandals, 24
Vereeniging, treaty of, 164
Versailles, treaty of, 190
Victoria, Lake, 10, 79, 83, 115, 143, 152, 154
Victoria, Queen, 179

Wainwright, Jacob, 178-79
Warri, 34
West African Frontier Force, 97
Wichale, treaty of, 101-02
Wilberforce, William, 56
Wilson, Woodrow, 107, 189, 197
World War I, 103-04, 196, 142, 155, 158, 165, 189, 191, 197, 205
World War II, 102-03, 142-43, 156, 158, 161, 181, 187, 193-94, 196-97, 205, 209-11, 214, 216, 219, 222

Xhosa, 53

Yoruba, 16, 97, 177
Young Kikuyu Association, 191

Zaghlul, Saad, 187
Zaire, 217
Zambezi River, 81

Zambia, 216
Zanaki, 213
Zanzibar, 10, 75, 82-3, 87, 96, 113, 118-19, 136, 143, 151, 179, 214, 216
Zelewski, Emil von, 112
Zimbabwe, 36